EGYPT HAS MORE WONDERS IN IT
THAN ANY OTHER COUNTRY IN THE WORLD,
AND MORE MONUMENTS THAT DEFY DESCRIPTION
THAN ANY OTHER PLACE.

– HERODOTUS

WHO WERE THE ANCIENT EGYPTIANS?

WHERE DID THEY COME FROM?

Studying the DNA of Egyptian mummies, scientists have discovered that the ancestors of the ancient Egyptians were European farmers who lived during the Neolithic age in the region of present-day Israel and Jordan. Around 6000 BC they migrated to the Nile Delta, bringing agriculture with them to Egypt. Even though the Ancient Egyptians settled on the African Continent, they were not related to native Africans.

WHAT LANGUAGE DID THEY SPEAK?

Ancient Egyptian language belongs to the family of Afro-Asiatic languages, spoken in the Middle East and North Africa. It is related to such languages as Phoenician (the source of all European alphabets), to Biblical and modern Hebrew spoken in Israel, to Aramaic that was spoken in Israel and Syria at the time of Christ, as well as to Arabic, the language of modern Egypt.

Ancient Egyptians used two types of writing – *hieroglyphic* and *hieratic* (cursive script used mostly for writing on papyrus). Later, during the Ptolemaic Period, they adopted a third type of writing, the *demotic* script. The Ancient Egyptian language was deciphered at the beginning of the 19th century through the study of an inscription on the famous Rosetta Stone – a text written in hieroglyphs and demotic script, and translated into Greek. Egyptian hieroglyphic writing is one of the most ancient on earth (second after Sumerian). The earliest known full sentence written in the Ancient Egyptian language dates to about 2690 BC.

THEIR LAND

The Ancient Egyptian civilization grew along the river Nile. The Nile flooded the land around it every year, depositing rich black mud wherever it's waters reached. The color of the Egyptian soil gave Egypt its ancient name – *Kemet* – the 'black land.' The name *Kemet* appears in such words as 'chemistry' and 'alchemy,' because ancient Europeans traced many fields of scientific knowledge to the science and magical arts of the Ancient Egyptians. The fertile soil and warm climate along the Nile allowed ancient farmers to cultivate crops year round. Agriculture became the backbone of Egypt's wealth.

HISTORICAL PERIODS AND INVENTIONS

The Bronze Age – when ancient people used copper and bronze in the making of tools and weapons – lasted from 3,300 to 1,200 BC. The Bronze Age saw the birth of civilizations and the development of advanced cultures in Europe, the Near East, and East Asia. By 3000 BC the Egyptians had invented the sail. Sea exploration and trade helped nurture their civilization. Since writing first appeared in the Bronze Age, it is the earliest period for which we have written documents and chronicles.

Egyptians made use of the pottery wheel from as early as 2600 BC, but the wheel was not used in transportation until 1000 years later. Horses and chariots were brought to Egypt by the Hyksos – invaders from the area of present-day Lebanon – between 1650 and 1550 BC.

The Bronze Age in Egypt lasted from around the construction of the pyramids to the era following Pharaoh Ramesses II – between 1200 and 1000 BC – when the Iron Age began.

Left: Queen Nefertari, wife of Pharaoh Ramesses II, playing senet (a game similar to chess) 1279–1213 BC
Below: "Egyptian Chess Players" by Lawrence Alma-Tadema
Gold "Eye of Horus" bracelet, Egypt, 943-922 BC

PHARAOH MENES AND PHARAOH NARMER

3200–3000 BC

The Narmer Palette, 3150 BC

Head of a pharaoh — possibly, Narmer

The Egyptians believed that the very first Egyptian pharaoh was Menes. However, most information about Menes comes to us from around 500 BC, and it's hard to separate historical truth from legend. Menes is similar to Romulus and Remus of Rome. He is a *cultural hero* more than a historical personality. Just like Romulus and Remus, Menes founded a city – Memphis, the ancient capital of Egypt. Greek historian Herodotus wrote that Menes built a giant dam and shifted the course of the Nile to make space for the new city.

In the legends of many ancient cultures we find the so-called *civilizing heroes* – humans or demi-gods whose mission was to teach people various skills vital for building a civilization – using fire, agriculture, writing, music, and so on. In Greek mythology, Prometheus gave mankind fire. In the Roman tradition, Numa Pompilius, the second king of Rome, learned about justice, law, and the sacred rites of worship from the nymph Egeria, and passed this knowledge to the Romans. Egyptian legends say that Menes received the throne of Egypt from the hands of the god Horus to bring people the gifts of civilization – the art of writing, the worship of gods, and even luxury!

Ancient Greek historian Diodorus Siculus who wrote in the 1st century BC, recorded the following legend in his book *Bibliotheca Historica – The Library of History*: "Menes taught the people to worship gods and offer sacrifices, and also to make tables and couches, and to use fancy bed sheets and blankets. So he is the person who introduced luxury and an extravagant lifestyle. And it is said that the descendants of this king, 52 in number, ruled one after another for more than 1040 years, but that in their reigns nothing happened that was worthy of writing down."

Ancient Greek historian Herodotus, the *Father of History*, who visited Egypt in the 5th century BC, wrote down the legend about King Menes and a crocodile. One day, while hunting on the banks of Lake Moeris, Menes was attacked by his own dogs. Just at that moment he spotted a crocodile in the lake and jumped onto its back. The crocodile took him to the opposite bank!

Diodorus Siculus adds to this story: "In gratitude to the beast he built a city, and called it Crocodilopolis, commanded crocodiles to be worshiped as gods, and dedicated the lake to them as a place for crocodiles to feed and multiply." Menes was not as lucky with hippos, though. According to the Egyptian historian Manetho (3rd century BC), after a reign of 62 years, Menes was killed by a wild hippopotamus.

Despite the fact that stories about Menes sound like myths, most historians think he was an actual historical figure. Some believe that 'Menes' was a title of the Pharaoh Narmer who lived around 3000 BC. Narmer married Princess Neithhotep of Lower Egypt, uniting Upper and Lower Egypt, and founding the 1st Dynasty of Egyptian kings. The famous Narmer Palette – a cosmetic palette used to grind and mix makeup pigments – shows Pharaoh Narmer fighting a battle to unify Egypt. It was carved from siltstone around 3200–3000 BC and found in a temple of the hawk-headed god Horus in Upper Egypt.

Greeks and Romans thought worshipping crocodiles was bizarre. "Most men are entirely at a loss to explain how these beasts that eat the flesh of men became sacred in Egypt," observes Diodorus, "and why it ever became the law to honor like the gods creatures of the most disgusting habits." When asked about their crocodile worship, according to Diodorus, the Egyptians pointed out that the crocodiles guard the Egyptian borders: "The robbers and criminals from Arabia and Libya do not dare to swim across the Nile for the fear of crocodiles."

"Egyptian priest reading a papyrus" by Stepan Bakalovich,

crocodile-headed god Sobek

Herodotus describes the worship of crocodiles: In every city Egyptians "keep one crocodile to which they do special honor. They train it to be tame, put earrings of glass and of gold into its ears, and bracelets on its feet, and feed it every day, and make offerings to it. And when it dies they make its body into a mummy and bury it in the sacred tombs."

Roman author Strabo, who visited Egypt in the 1st century AD, during the reign of the Emperor Augustus, was invited by his Egyptian host to offer treats to a sacred crocodile. Strabo's host "brought with him from the supper table a small cake, spiced meat, and a small jar of honey and milk. The crocodile was lying on the edge of the lake. One of the priests opened its mouth, another put the cake into it, then the meat, and afterward poured down the honey and milk." Sounds like the croc was annoyed, because it leaped into the lake and crossed to the other side. But the worshippers kept arriving with more treats. "When another visitor came with his offering," continues Strabo, "the priests took the food, went around the lake, caught the crocodile again and repeated the process of feeding."

A pharaoh hunting a hippopotamus

Ancient Egyptians believed that many animals were connected to gods. For example, when a black calf was born, says Herodotus, that had "a square mark of white on its forehead, and on its back the shape of an eagle, and if the hair on its tail was long, people put on their best clothes and celebrated, saying that a god has come down to live among them."

Diodorus Siculus recorded a fascinating legend that seeks to explain the origin of animal worship in Egypt. "The early Egyptians were often defeated in battles because of the lack of order in their army. So they came up with the idea of carrying standards – military banners – before their troops. The standards were figures of animals attached to spears – a different animal for each unit, so that every soldier knew where his place was. And since good order contributed to victory, they thought that the animals were responsible for their success."

"Worship of the god Ra"
by Edward John Poynter

Ancient Egyptian sandals

"A priestess feeding
the sacred ibis birds"
by Edwin Longsden Long

PHARAOH DJOSER

REIGNED 2686 -2648 BC

The time in Egyptian history when the Egyptian state was organized around a pharaoh and his government is called the *Dynastic Period*. It is divided into three *kingdoms* with *intermediate periods* in between –
the Old Kingdom (2686 – 2181 BC),
the Middle Kingdom (2055 – 1650 BC), and
the New Kingdom (1550 – 1069 BC).
During the Dynastic Period, Egypt was ruled by 30 dynasties – or families – of pharaohs. The Old Kingdom includes the period when the Egyptian pyramids were built. It spans about 200 years (2691-2504 BC) – from the reign of Pharaoh Djoser of the 3rd dynasty through the reign of Pharaoh Menkaure of the 4th dynasty.
Since ancient Egyptian documents and chronicles indicate dates by counting years of pharaohs' reigns ("in the fifth year of his reign..."), and we don't know exactly when this or that pharaoh ruled, most dates in Egyptian history are approximate. For some periods they are plus-or-minus 300 years.

A pharaoh was the head of the Egyptian state. His government was run by a *vizir*, the chief minister, who employed a great number of officials and scribes to carry out government tasks, such as managing the treasury, defense, taxation, and building projects. The priests of major Egyptian temples had also a lot of influence on the pharaoh. They were the guardians of technical and scientific knowledge in many fields, such as agriculture, medicine, engineering, astronomy, and history.

Pharaoh Djoser was one of the early Old Kingdom pharaohs. His name means 'the Powerful.'
He was the first to secure the borders of Egypt from unwelcome migrations and attacks. Once Egypt was safe, he moved to conquer some foreign lands. When a 7-year-long drought caused a famine in Egypt, Djoser ordered the rebuilding of the Temple of Khnum, the god that represented the source of the Nile River. According to the inscription on the Famine Stela built during the Ptolemaic dynasty, the god Khnum took pity on the people of Egypt and stopped the drought.

Manetho says that Pharaoh Djoser ruled for 29 years. "Among the Egyptians," he writes, "he is compared to Asclepius (the Greek god of medicine) in recognition of his medical skill.

The inventor of the art of building with cut stone, he also pursued the craft of writing." "The art of building with cut stone" refers to the world's oldest stone monument, the Step Pyramid, constructed during Djoser's reign, and still standing today.

The 203-feet-high Step Pyramid was built of huge limestone blocks between 2630 BC and 2611 BC in Saqqara, northwest of the city of Memphis. Underneath the pyramid there is an underground labyrinth – 6 kilometers of tunnels and vast chambers on many levels cut into the bedrock. The Step Pyramid was designed by Imhotep, the first man in history to be described as a professional architect. Before Imhotep, buildings in Egypt were constructed of sun-baked mud bricks, or of small natural stones. Imhotep turned to cutting stone from the bedrock and shaping stone blocks to fit his design. He is also believed to have invented an irrigation system to bring water from the Nile to Memphis.

"Building the Pyramids" by Peter Jackson; right: a mummy case from around 1600 BC

Recently engineers made an interesting observation about the structure of the Step Pyramid. Imhotep used palm tree trunks to support the stones of the ceiling inside the burial chamber. The ancient wood started crumbling. To repair the ceiling, engineers drilled holes into the walls of the burial chamber. Some holes were 4 meters (12 feet) long, but the drill never reached the huge limestone blocks covering the surface of the pyramid. The walls seemed to be filled with small stones. The idea that the pyramid is built entirely of huge blocks is wrong, concluded the engineers. The body of the pyramid is a pile of rubble and smaller stones, covered on the outside with the giant limestone blocks.

Egyptologists believe the Step Pyramid was built as the Pharaoh's tomb. The burial chamber is connected to a stairway by which the spirit of the Pharaoh was supposed to leave the pyramid and rise to the stars. Some researchers, however, say the vast underground portion of the pyramid is too sophisticated and complex for a tomb. The 'burial chamber' is a granite-walled room 28 meters (90 feet) high, located 4 levels under the pyramid. Inside, there is a gigantic 15-feet-high precision-cut box made from 32 granite blocks that weigh between 3 and 10 tons each. The blocks are fitted together with astonishing accuracy without any glue or mortar. Is that box indeed a *sarcophagus* – the pharaoh's coffin – or was it built for some other purpose?

Above: a hallway inside the Step Pyramid
Left: the 'sarcophagus' inside the Step Pyramid
Below: clothing of pharaohs and their guards

PHARAOH KHUFU

2589–2566 BC

Pharaoh Khufu (also known under a Greek name, Cheops) ruled about a century after Djoser. The greatest achievement of his reign is considered to be the Great Pyramid of Giza – one of the Seven Wonders of the ancient world. 147 meters high (481 feet), it remained the tallest building in the world for about 3,800 years, until the construction of the Lincoln Cathedral in England, in AD 1311. Ironically, the only known statue of Khufu is the smallest statue of any pharaoh in the history of Egypt – less than three inches tall!

Herodotus portrays Khufu as a tyrant. He writes: "This king did very wickedly, forbidding the people to do sacrifice to the gods, and making them work on his building projects. For it was this Cheops that built the greatest of the pyramids. First he made a causeway for the carrying of the stones. And these stones were cut from quarries in the Arabian hills, and being drawn to the river were carried across by men appointed for that purpose. The number of those that worked was one hundred thousand men, and when they had labored for three months there came another hundred thousand. The causeway was ten years in building and the pyramid twenty. And when it was finished there was written an inscription on it, saying how much had been spent on radishes, onions, and garlic for the builders, and the sum was sixteen hundred talents of silver."

Above right: Egyptian stone vase, 3rd millennium BC
Right: "The building of the pyramids" by Max Thedy

The building of the pyramids

The idea that the pyramids were built by slaves is likely incorrect. The excavations around the pyramids indicate that the teams of pyramid builders were probably skilled full-time construction workers assisted by farmers during the season when there was not much agricultural work. In addition to the "radishes, onions, and garlic" mentioned by Herodotus, ancient *papyri* (plural of *papyrus*) say that the pyramid-builders ate dates, vegetables, poultry, and meat (foods not available to slaves), drank beer, and were paid in goods and even land.

The Westcar Papyrus (18th-16th centuries BC), also known as *King Cheops and the Magicians*, contains a few stories supposedly told at the court of Pharaoh Khufu. Khufu wanted to learn the secrets of the temple of the ibis-headed god Thoth, and use that knowledge to build his own tomb. He hoped to find a wizard who could tell him the number of rooms in the Temple of Thoth. One of Khufu's sons told the pharaoh: "There is a man by the name of Dedi, who is 110 years old. Every day he eats 500 cakes, and a leg of beef, and drinks 100 pots of beer. If you cut a head off an animal, Dedi can attach it back to the body and make the animal alive again!" Khufu had Dedi brought to his palace. "Is it true," he asked, "that you can reattach the head that has been cut off from the body?" Dedi answered, "It's true." "Bring here a prisoner," ordered the king, "so that his death sentence may be carried out right here." But the magician asked permission to show his magic on an animal, not on a human being.

So they brought a goose, and cut off its head. Dedi said his magical spells, and the body of the goose stood up and waddled towards its head, the head leaped onto the body, and the goose stood up on its legs and cackled.

Seeing that Dedi was a real magician, Khufu asked him: "Do you know the number of rooms in the Temple of Thoth?" Dedi replied, "No. But I know where to find the secrets of Thoth. They are hidden in Heliopolis, in a box made of flint." The king ordered him to bring the box. "O king my lord," said Dedi, "we can't open the box with the secrets of Thoth."

"Who can?" asked the pharaoh.

"The oldest of the three children of Reddjedet."

"Who is Reddjedet?"

"She is the wife of a priest of the god Ra. Her oldest son will become the pharaoh and rule this land, but he is not born yet."

The king became sad. He realized that Dedi had just predicted the change of dynasty. "Don't be sad," Dedi told him. "Your son will rule after you, and then your son's son, but after him the throne will go to the children of Reddjedet."

Khufu belonged to the 4th Dynasty. *The Westcar Papyrus* was created during the reign of the 5th Dynasty. The story was clearly composed to justify the transfer of royal power to a new family. The papyrus portrays Khufu as a cruel ruler, while the pharaohs of the next dynasty are portrayed as kind to their people.

Head band, Egypt, 2600–2500 BC, gold, carnelian, and lapis lazuli

Was Khufu, indeed, the builder of the Great Pyramid? In Ancient Egypt royal names were usually written inside cartouches. *Cartouche* is French for 'cartridge.' In hieroglyphic writing it's an oval with a line at one end. Khufu's name inside his cartouche was spelled with 4 hieroglyphs: a circle, a quail, a snake, a quail. The official name of Khufu's tomb was *Akhet Khufu* – Khufu's Horizon, but was that tomb the Great Pyramid of Giza? Inside the pyramid there are no statues, reliefs, or inscriptions. A box carved from a solid block of red granite – believed to be Khufu's sarcophagus – was found empty in the pyramid burial chamber.

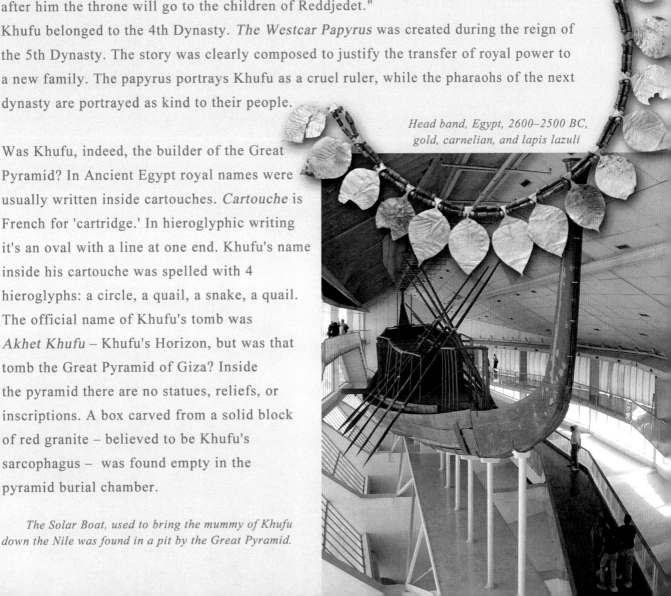

The Solar Boat, used to bring the mummy of Khufu down the Nile was found in a pit by the Great Pyramid.

If the Great Pyramid was indeed built during the reign of Khufu, how did ancient Egyptians bring 2.3 million stone blocks, each weighing more than two tons from a quarry many miles away? They didn't have the wheel when they built the pyramids. How did they cut the limestone and granite for the pyramid using only the Bronze Age copper tools? They didn't have iron or steel. How did they lift the giant blocks and fit them to a hair's breadth block to block? How did they manage to align the sides of the pyramid to the four cardinal directions with unbelievable accuracy?

One theory suggests that the ancient Egyptians moved massive stone blocks on sleds by pouring water on the sand in front of sleds to reduce friction. Another theory is that they used log rollers, but to move the 2.3 million blocks they would have used up all the trees in Egypt to the last tree! Another traditional explanation is that to lift stone blocks they used a spiral ramp outside the pyramid. The problem with this explanation is that to finish the pyramid during the reign of Khufu, the builders had to lift a block and put it in place about every three minutes. And there is no way ramps could hold the numbers of men needed to pull many stones at the same time.

One alternative theory says that the stone blocks were not cut in a quarry. They were created by pouring thick limestone cement into forms positioned on the pyramid. Natural Egyptian limestone contains 96-99% calcite, but the pyramid blocks contain only 85-90% calcite, as well as minerals not found in natural limestone. Also, unlike natural limestone, the pyramid stone is full of tiny air bubbles. In addition, in the pyramid limestone larger bits of prehistoric fossils are always found at the bottom of pyramid blocks – as if they sank to the bottom during the pouring of cement.

Below: megalithic walls in Sacsayhuamán, Peru
Right: Angkor Wat, Cambodia

Ancient prehistoric structures built of enormous stones are called *megalithic* (from Greek *mega* – 'large' + *lithos* 'stone'). Megalithic constructions are found on all continents. There are also mysterious legends about ancient building techniques including techniques for softening stone. Legends of the Inca tribe of Peru say that the gods gave ancient people a substance that could melt stone. Megalithic structures in Sacsayhuaman, Peru, built thousands of years before the Inca, look as if they were molded into complex shapes and put together like a puzzle. They fit together so precisely that you can't even slide a sheet of paper between the stones. In Southeast Asia, the temples of Angkor Wat, Cambodia, are said to have been built by a demi-god who used magical water to soften the rocks and give them form before they hardened again.

But even the theory of using limestone cement to create the giant blocks of Khufu's pyramid cannot explain the 8000 tons of granite blocks that were used to create the walls and ceilings of chambers inside the pyramid. These blocks match stone from the quarries in Aswan – over 500 miles (860 km) away.

shafts

king's chamber

grand gallery

queen's chamber

underground chamber

dead end

escape shaft

entrance

Left: the chambers, passages and shafts inside the Great Pyramid of Khufu
Above: giant stone blocks of the Great Pyramid

PHARAOH KHAFRE

REIGNED AROUND 2570 BC

Khafre was the son of Khufu and most Egyptologists consider him the builder of the second largest pyramid of Giza – 10 feet shorter than the pyramid of Khufu. Herodotus didn't have a high opinion of Khafre: "...And after Khufu, Khafre reigned fifty years and six months, and behaved himself in the same wicked way, oppressing the people and forbidding them to worship the gods."

Just like Khufu's pyramid, Khafre's pyramid houses a chamber with a huge stone box – believed to be a sarcophagus. However, there is no evidence that Khafre was ever buried there. There are no inscriptions or statues inside the pyramid. In the 19th century, in a deep water-filled well not far from the Sphynx, they found a few statues of Khafre, thrown into the well in ancient times – all headless except one. Clearly Khafre was not everybody's favorite pharaoh!

The Great Sphinx – a giant statue carved from a single mass of limestone over an underground network of chambers and tunnels – is said to date to the time of Khafre as well. It is close to Khafre's pyramid temple complex, and some see a certain resemblance between the faces of the Sphinx and Khafre as portrayed in his statues.

The Great Sphinx and the sarcophagus of Khafre

With the head of a human wearing a royal headdress, and the body of a lion, the Sphinx may have been created as a guardian of Khafre's pyramid, and a symbol of royal power. The name *Sphinx* was given to the statue by Greek travelers. It refers to the monster of Greek mythology – a beast with the head of a woman, the body of a lion, and the wings of an eagle. Egyptians called the Sphinx *Horemakhet* – 'Horus of the Horizon.' Horus is the ancient Egyptian god of the sky and royal power usually depicted with the head of a falcon.

Not everyone thinks that the Sphinx was built for Pharaoh Khafre. Some researchers point out that the erosion of the limestone around the Sphinx looks like it was caused by hundreds of years of heavy rainfall. But the last time North Africa experienced heavy rainfalls was around 7000 BC. The limestone could not be weathered by winds, because for most of its history the Sphinx was buried in the sand up to its shoulders. Also the lines of erosion around the Sphinx are vertical, while wind erosion creates only horizontal bands.

Some researchers focus on the fact that the head of the Sphinx looks too small for its body. They believe that originally the Sphinx had the head of a lion (later re-carved into the head of a pharaoh) and that it was created long before Egyptian civilization – in prehistoric times, around 10,500 BC, when on the spring equinox the Sun rose in the constellation of Leo.

Other critics of the supposed Sphinx-Khafre connection remind us that of the hundreds of hieroglyphic inscriptions in the tombs of Giza dating back to the reign of Khafre, not a single one mentions the Sphinx. The Inventory Stela from the 7th century BC records a legend that the Sphinx was only found by Khufu, buried in the sand, and not built by Khufu or Khafre.

Above: "The Sphinx buried in the sand" - 19th century
Right: vertical erosion pattern on the walls of the Sphinx enclosure

Egyptologists explain the lack of evidence that Khafre was buried in his pyramid by the fact that most ancient tombs were robbed. Some were robbed by thieves, and others by pharaohs of later dynasties who stole treasures and statues from ancient burials to place them in their own tombs. Theft was common in Ancient Egypt - like anywhere in the world, throughout history. And it's likely that Egyptian laws were not severe to thieves. Diodorus Siculus describes a bizarre law about theft in ancient Egypt: "The Egyptian law dealing with thieves required that every thief register his name with an official called 'the Chief of the Thieves' and bring to him all the stolen items. Meanwhile, anyone who had been robbed filed with the Chief of the Thieves a list of all the missing items, stating the place, the day, and the hour of the loss. And since all the stolen articles were instantly found, the owner paid one-fourth of the value of the stolen goods and got them back. It was said that this law was created, because it was impossible to stop people from stealing."

The Sphinx was excavated and cleaned of sand three times in its history. The first was between 1401–1391 BC, during the reign of Pharaoh Thutmose IV. Thutmose IV became the pharaoh against the will of his father who appointed Thutmose's brother as the crown prince. To justify capturing the throne, Thutmose IV came up with the story of a miracle recorded on the so-called Dream Stele – a carved stone tablet standing between the paws of the Sphinx. The Dream Stele is the first recorded mention of the Sphinx.

Right: Dream Stele
Below: courtyard of an Egyptian palace

"One day, before he had ascended to the throne of Egypt," says the Dream Stele story, "Thutmose IV was hunting alone in the desert. It was noon, and the sun beat fiercely down upon him, so that he sought the shadow between the paws of the Sphinx. Great and powerful was the god, and very majestic was his image, with the face of a man and the body of a lion, a snake upon his brow. In many temples sacrifices were made to him, in many towns did men worship with their faces turned toward him. The king fell asleep and in his sleep saw the Sphinx open its lips and speak to him. It was no longer a thing of motionless rock, but the god himself, the great Harmachis. And he addressed the dreamer saying,

"Behold me, O Thutmose, for I am the Sun god, the ruler of all people. Harmachis is my name, and Ra, and Khepera, and Tem. I am your father, and you are my son, and through me shall all good come to you if you listen to my words. The land of Egypt will be yours, both the North Land, and the South Land. In prosperity and happiness you will rule for many years." He paused, and it seemed to Thutmose that the god was struggling to free himself from the overwhelming sands, for only his head was visible.

"As you see," Harmachis continued, "the sands of the desert are over me. Do that quickly which I command you, O my son Thuthmose."

The remainder of the inscription on the Dream Stele is damaged, but it's likely that it records the Sphinx ordering Thutmose to excavate him from the sands.

The Sphinx was excavated a second time by the Romans, following the Roman conquest of Egypt, and finally a third time by European archaeologists in the 19th century.

Above: bracelets of Queen Hetepheres, 2575 – 2528 BC
Left: "A temple procession" by Frederick Arthur Bridgman

PHARAOH MENKAURE

REIGNED STARTING 2530 BC

Pharaoh Menkaure (also known under his Greek name, Mycerinus) was the son of Kafre. He built the third – and the smallest – Pyramid in Giza. In the basalt box – the sarcophagus – inside the pyramid they discovered a mummy, but the radio carbon test dated the mummy to the early centuries AD. So it wasn't the body of Menkaure. Unfortunately, the sarcophagus was lost when the ship which was transporting it to England sank.

Herodotus describes Menkaure as being opposed to Khufu's and Khafre's cruelty. He says that Menkaure brought peace and respect back to Egypt. "When Khufu was dead, there reigned his son, Menkaure by name. This man walked not in the ways of his father, but opened the temples, and was kind to the people, allowing them to go about their own business... Also he gave more righteous judgment in all matters than any of the kings of Egypt before him. Nevertheless Menkaure experienced a lot of grief. First of all his daughter died, his only child... Then came to him an oracle from the city of Buto that he should live six years only, and die in the seventh. The King was very angry, and sent messengers to that temple, saying, 'How come my father oppressed the people, yet the gods gave him a long life? I am righteous, but I must die in my youth!' But the oracle answered him again, saying, 'You will die because you do something you shouldn't do. The will of the gods is that Egypt should suffer for 150 years.' When King Menkaure heard it, he made a lot of lamps and had them lit all night. He held feasts that lasted day and night! 'If I live not only the days but the nights also, then I will live not six but twelve years,' he figured."

Below: "Weighing of the heart"
from the Egyptian Book of the Dead, 1050 BC
Left: a sphinx statue in the fields near Memphis

"An Egyptian feast" by Edwin Longsden Long

The legend says that Pharaoh Menkaure spent the last 6 years of his life in never-ending feasts and parties. While traveling in Egypt, Herodotus observed an interesting custom related to the idea that 'you only have one life to live.' "The rich men among the Egyptians have this custom at their feasts. At the end of the meal they carry around a painted wooden sculpture of a man in a coffin. The host brings it to each guest at the table, repeating these words: 'Drink and enjoy, because this is what you will be when you die.'"

Below: Wrapping a mummy; Right: a gold ring with a turquoise bead, Egypt, 1850–1640 BC

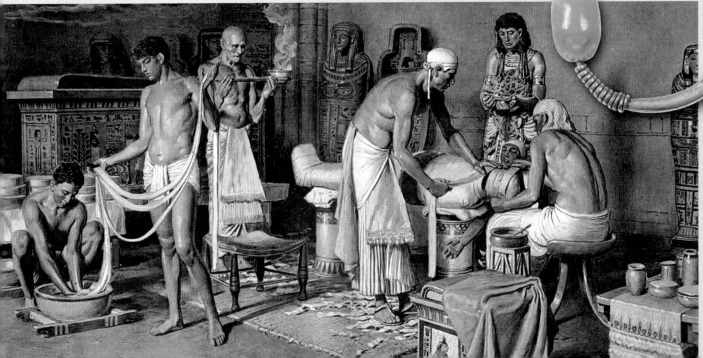

Ancient historians praised King Menkaure for his justice and kindness. Poets were fascinated with the image of a man facing unjust punishment for taking the side of his people. Below are two stanzas from the poem "Mycerinus" by the 19th-century English poet Matthew Arnold:

"My father loved injustice, and lived long,
Crowned with grey hairs he died, and full of sway.
I loved the good he scorned, and hated wrong –
The gods declare my recompense today.
I looked for life more lasting, rule more high,
And when six years are measured, lo, I die! ...

Into the silence of the groves and woods
I will go forth; though something would I say –
Something – yet what, I know not; for the gods
The doom they pass revoke not, nor delay;
And prayers, and gifts, and tears, are fruitless all,
And the night waxes, and the shadows fall..."

Menkaure's pyramid shares with the Great Pyramid one fascinating feature. In 1940 a British Air Force pilot flying over Giza noticed something strange about the Great Pyramid – something nobody had ever noticed before. He took a picture. In the picture you can clearly see that the pyramid is not a 4-sided, but an 8-sided structure. Each side has an indentation running from the top to the base (4'-deep at the base) splitting each face of the pyramid into two surfaces tilted toward each other. Menkaure's pyramid has the same structure. The 8 facets of these pyramids are visible from above, but from the ground they can only be seen at sunrise and sunset on the spring and autumn equinoxes, when the rays of the sun 'split' each side of the pyramids into two.

To create such 8-sided shapes the ancient Egyptian builders had to have an extraordinary degree of precision in their engineering and building techniques. Why would they have doubled their work for a feature which nobody could see?

Above: "Carrying a pharaoh's mummy across the Nile"; gold strainer, Egypt, 1279 – 1213 BC
Left: Aerial photo of the pyramids from 1940

EGYPTOLOGISTS vs ENGINEERS

Egyptology is the study of ancient Egyptian history and culture. Traditionally, Egyptologists were academics – university professors. But as Egyptology became widely popular in the 20th century through new archaeological discoveries, travel, documentaries, and, finally, the internet, it attracted new researchers who were not professors. Some of them were engineers who approached the mysteries of the pyramids and the Sphinx using their expertise in science, construction, architecture, and other fields. Suddenly, many ideas that academic Egyptologists had never questioned, were reviewed and criticized.

A deep split occurred between university professors – Egyptologists and archaeologists – and researchers with science and engineering expertise. Academics doing Egyptology research as a career have to be careful. If they express ideas that contradict the opinions of their teachers and colleagues, they may lose opportunities to publish their works in prestigious magazines or to be promoted to leading positions in their university departments. Unlike the academics, the engineers and scientists are not paid or praised for their Egyptology research. They do it to satisfy their curiosity. They don't care whether their ideas are accepted by their colleagues. These engineers are rebels for whom Egyptology research is an adventure. Below I will outline a few areas where academic archaeologists and Egyptologists clash with engineers and scientists.

1. Some researchers with engineering expertise suggest that the ancient Egyptians didn't have the technology necessary to build the great pyramids of Egypt and the Sphinx. Who built the pyramids? Perhaps a more technologically advanced civilization that perished at the end of the last Ice Age, around the 11th century BC – long before the Egyptians. The legend of Atlantis – a highly-developed ancient civilization that perished without a trace – is often quoted. Perhaps the Egyptians found the pyramids built by a prehistoric civilization and used them as tombs. They may have added the outer white 'casing' stones and restored some portions of the pyramids but were not the original builders, say the engineers.

The Unfinished Obelisk in the Aswan granite quarry, Egypt. Cut around the 15th century BC, it would have stood 137 feet tall and weighed 1168 tons. Egyptologists say ancient stone workers cut it using balls of dolerite (which is harder than granite). Really?

If you compare the precision of the stone-cutting and building of the most ancient Egyptian monuments to the work of later eras, it looks like the Egyptians were not improving their techniques – they were gradually losing them. The building blocks were getting smaller and smaller, they were no longer as precisely fit, nor as beautifully polished.

There are other megalithic structures, including pyramids, in many parts of the world – in Central and South America, in Europe and in Asia. There is still no explanation how ancient people were able to build sophisticated structures without advanced engineering and machines. That's what many engineers claim.

Academic Egyptologists and archaeologists disagree, and find these ideas laughable. How could an advanced civilization disappear without a trace, leaving no writing, no tools, or information about their culture?

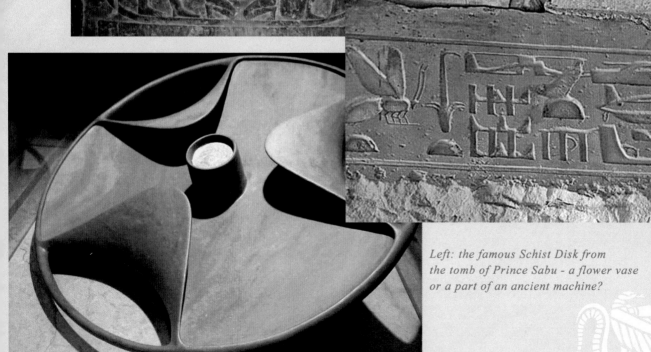

Above: stone bowl, Egypt, 2573-2454 BC.

Lost ancient technology?..
Left: a mysterious image looking like a light bulb from the Dendera Temple complex in Egypt
Below: strange shapes looking like flying machines from a relief in the Temple of Seti in Abydos, Egypt

Left: the famous Schist Disk from the tomb of Prince Sabu - a flower vase or a part of an ancient machine?

2. The *sarcophagi* (Latin plural of *sarcophagus* – coffin) – or the stone boxes inside the pyramids – are cut from multi-ton solid chunks of granite or basalt and polished smooth as glass. Engineers claim Ancient Egyptians could not have cut granite with the primitive tools of the Bronze Age – copper chisels and dolerite pounding stones. The hardest substance is diamond, but diamond blades and diamond-tip tools capable of cutting any stone were invented only in the 19th century. Researchers point to saw and drill marks visible on the stone boxes – the traces of tools that Ancient Egyptians did not have.

In underground vaults, 33 meters below the Step Pyramid, archaeologists found over 40,000 stone vessels – cups, dishes, and vases – cut from some of the hardest types of stone, such as granite, quartz, and diorite. The vessels are perfectly smooth outside and inside, and their sides are extremely thin, often semi-transparent. That couldn't be done with copper chisels, say the engineers. In addition, most vessels are perfectly symmetric. They look as if they were created by a machine that rotated them as they were cut, drilled, and sanded, but in the days of Pharaoh Djoser Egyptians didn't yet have the wheel.

Is it possible that the stone boxes and the stone vessels were created way before Ancient Egypt, by some technologically advanced civilization? If they were created by the Ancient Egyptians, why didn't the Egyptian craftsmen create stone lids for them? The precision-cut jars and vases under the Step Pyramid were sealed with plugs made from mud!

The opponents of this theory argue that the Egyptians used sand (containing quartz which is harder than copper). They suggest the Egyptians poured sand on a block of hard stone, such as granite, basalt, or diorite, along the line where the cut was to be made, then pulled a copper saw back-and-forth endlessly. It was the sand that cut the stone, not the copper saw, Egyptologists say.

Stone jars and vases found under the Step Pyramid

Below: Another unsolved mystery – keystone cuts with metal poured into them to create clamps are found in prehistoric megalithic structures all over the world. Global ancient civilization?

Giant precision-cut granite boxes in the underground temple Serapeum in Saqqara: Sarcophagi of the sacred Apis bulls or containers used for chemical reactions by the ancient technologists?

Each sarcophagus weighs 70-100 tons. Each one was carved in place, underground, from a single block of granite, and polished to mirror shine. All this work to bury a mummified bull!

The Serapeum is a system of passages and vaults. There are no traces of fire on the ceiling or walls. What kind of light was used by the creators of the Serapeum? Egyptologists say it could be a system of mirrors. Hmmm...

3. The pyramids weren't tombs, say the engineers. And the stone boxes inside them weren't sarcophagi (coffins). No pharaoh mummies or treasures were found in any of the three great pyramids. Even the wide-spread theft of ancient treasures cannot explain the absence of any hieroglyphic inscriptions in any of the great pyramids. Nor do they appear on the Sphinx. There was only one inscription found in Khufu's pyramid indicating that it was the tomb of Khufu. That inscription is now believed to be a 19th-century fake created by a British archaeologist who tried to generate excitement to secure funding for his expeditions to Egypt.

Perhaps the pyramids and the Sphinx were not built by the pharaohs but just discovered by them. Perhaps these monuments had been sealed so well that the pharaohs had no access to their chambers and underground passages and therefore left no inscriptions on the walls to claim them.

Engineers argue that whenever Egyptologists come across a structure whose function they don't understand, they call it a temple or a tomb. Inside the pyramids there are mysterious chambers made from the hardest stone, and narrow vents that cut through the mass of the pyramids with astonishing precision. Engineers believe that these features are too sophisticated and precise to have been built for dead pharaohs, they must have had some technical function. So, if pyramids were not tombs, what was their function? The conjectures range from astronomical observatories to power plants or water pumps that used now lost technologies.

Egyptologists say such ideas are pure science fiction, not history.

Engineers say the drill holes and scoops found in ancient Egyptian stonework could have been made only by power tools!

4. Engineers wonder why ancient Egyptians stopped building pyramids, and why their most impressive work was done during the Old Kingdom – at the beginning of the Egyptian civilization, and not later. Somehow, according to the academic Egyptologists, the Egyptians went from the Stone Age to building the giant pyramids within only 3 to 4 generations, rapidly developing their incredible building and stone-cutting technology. And then, during the following two thousand years they stopped building the pyramids, lost the technique of building megalithic structures, their work becoming less and less sophisticated...? Why were the most ancient 'sarcofagi' – stone boxes – created with incredible precision techniques – with perfectly straight angles, flawless symmetry, and mirror-like polish, while the coffins from the later eras of Egyptian civilization were cut with primitive tools and look rough and unfinished? Why did they stop creating the amazing stone vessels, like the ones found under Djoser's pyramid, and, instead, went back to primitive clay pottery? That's not how civilizations develop. So far Egyptologists have not offered any solutions to this mystery.

5. Some ancient Egyptian artifacts – objects from the earliest times of Egyptian civilization – are known as *out-of-place artifacts* – items that look like they don't belong to their historical era. One such object is the famous Schist Disk – a circular 24-inch-wide object carved of schist stone. Engineers insist that this disk looks like a part of a machine.
No, it's just a flower vase, say the Egyptologists.

Aside from the arguments about its purpose, researchers are puzzled with the technique used to manufacture such an object. Schist is a layered and very brittle stone. It cannot be carved into a complex shape like this without immediately breaking. Was the stone first somehow softened, and then bent and folded? Most of the Egyptian schist objects had been made before the pyramids were built. For some reason this material was never used in later periods. Was the technique of working with brittle stone lost and forgotten?

Yet another mystery! Strange 'knobs' on megalithic blocks found around the world! Examples: Menkaure's pyramid; Delphi, Greece; Cusco, Peru

QUEEN HATSHEPSUT

REIGNED 1479 – 1458 BC

Hatshepsut began her rule as a queen married to Pharaoh Thutmose II. After her husband's death she became the *regent* (a grownup guardian and co-ruler) of her 2-year-old stepson Thutmose III. However, instead of guarding the throne for her stepson, this 'evil stepmother' went on and proclaimed herself a pharaoh, using everything – from dressup to deception – to rule Egypt as 'king' (not queen)! Here is the story of Hatshepsut.

Around 1710 BC some tribes from the Levant (the area of present-day Syria, Israel and Lebanon) known as the Hyksos migrated to the Nile Delta. Within 30 years their population grew and they started a war to take over Egypt. They had a huge advantage over the Egyptians: They had horses and the wheel – which the Egyptians didn't have at that time. So they attacked Egyptians with war chariots! In 1680 BC the Hyksos took over the Northern part of Egypt and ruled it as pharaohs for about 100 years.

A legend recorded around 1200 BC reported the humiliation of Egyptian pharaohs during the rule of the Hyksos. The Hyksos King Apophis sent to the pharaoh in Thebes (the ancient capital of Egypt in the area of present-day Luxor) an insulting message saying that the noise made by the hippos in Thebes was disturbing to King Apophis – four hundred miles away in the Delta! Unwilling to be ruled by the foreigners, the native Egyptian kings in Thebes raised an army and eventually liberated their land from the Hyksos.

Right: "The expulsion of the Hyksos"
Left: "Frog" ring, Egypt, 1353-1357 BC

*"The temple at Philae"
by Henry Hardinge
Cunynghame
Below: mirror,
Egypt, 1479-1425 BC*

However, the war was long, and as Egyptian warlords were away fighting the enemy
for weeks and months, they relied on their women to keep Upper Egypt under control.
That's how the wives and daughters of Egyptian rulers gained greater authority than before.

Hatshepsut's father, Thutmose I, was a general in the wars against the Hyksos. His name means
'Born of the God Thoth.' Having become the pharaoh, he expanded the borders of Egypt deep
into the Levant and captured the gold mines of Nubia. When Hatshepsut became a teenager,
Thutmose I named her Egypt's highest priestess – the God's Wife of Amun. In this role,
Hatshepsut was not allowed to get married and have a family. Instead, she spent her days in
secret sacred rituals, chanting prayers and walking around temples in endless processions.
She also managed her own palace, lands, treasury, and a staff of hundreds of priests, scribes,
and farmers. But everything changed for Hatshepsut with the death of her father Thutmose I.
Hatshepsut's brother, Thutmose II, became king, and Hatshepsut was selected to become his queen.

The practice of marrying close relatives (siblings or cousins) existed in many ruling dynasties
of the ancient world. If the king's wife was from his family, he didn't have to share power and
wealth with the family of the queen. However, marriages between close relatives result in genetic
damage. The kids born in such marriages may have incurable genetic diseases, body deformities,
and mental problems. Ancient Egyptians were unaware of this medical truth. Pharaohs often
married their sisters, which resulted in their kids' poor health and early deaths.

In addition, half of all kids in Egypt died before the age of 5 from malaria, food poisoning,
infectious diseases, and accidents. To increase chances that at least one of their sons survives

to adulthood, pharaohs had more than one wife, and many kids. One of the wives was named the Royal Wife, the pharaoh's queen. But even if she gave birth to a son it was not guaranteed that her son would become the next king. The heir to the throne was selected by an oracle, in a special secret ritual. The high priests of Amun brought out the statue of the god Amun from its shrine. It was standing in a wooden boat which the priests carried on their shoulders. The king, or his vizir asked the oracle a question, and the statue turned to indicate its answer. Of course, the statue didn't move on its own. The priests of Amun manipulated the statue to answer the question in this or that way.

Hatshepsut married her brother Thutmose II and became his Royal Wife. They had a daughter. Following tradition, Thutmose II had other wives too. Some of them gave birth to sons. But only after about 3 years of reign Thutmose II suddenly died. His kids were 1- and 2-year-olds. Who would become the next king? The priests of Amun held the oracle ceremony. The sons of the dead pharaoh were seated in a great sacred hall at Amun's temple, and the priests carried the Amun statue, circling around the hall, as if taking a close look at each boy. Finally the high priest announced that the god Amun had selected one of the princes. Two-year-old Thutmose III was to be the next pharaoh. His mother was from a family that didn't have much wealth and influence. There was a reason for this choice. Hatshepsut and the high priests felt it would be easier to manipulate a king who was not surrounded by a powerful family. Usually, if a child became pharaoh, his mother acted as the regent – a co-ruler of the king – until he grew up. But Hatshepsut didn't want to share power with Isis, the future king's mother. Hatshepsut broke the rule and proclaimed herself the regent of Thutmose III. She also erased the name of her husband Thutmose II from the monuments they had erected together, and replaced his name – with her own name.

"The Worship of the lunar god Khonsu" by Wladyslaw Bakalowicz

Hutshepsut as king

As before, Hatshepsut's days were filled with secret rituals, temple processions, and chanting. But her position as a regent was weak, so she was forced to share power with priests and the elite – the top families of Egypt. Had she refused, they would have replaced her as regent with Isis – the new king's mother. The families closest to the throne ran the show. We know this, because during Hatshepsut's reign these families started building for themselves palaces and tombs that were much more grand and luxurious than ever before.

One of Hatshepsut's officials, Ineni, placed in his tomb an inscription praising Hatshepsut: "The Wife of Amun, Hatshepsut, fulfilled the needs of the land. Egypt was obedient. The two banks of the Nile were content with her speech. Her majesty praised me, and she loved me. She knew my excellence in the palace. She provided me with things, and she made me great."

The elite Egyptian families that supported Hatshepsut enjoyed so much power that they were not looking forward to the time when Thutmose III would grow up and rule on his own. They started thinking of ways to make Hatshepsut's rule permanent. When Thutmose III was about 5 years old, Hatshepsut sent one of her government officials, Senenmut, to a red granite quarry in Aswan

to oversee the cutting of two giant 10-story obelisks for Thutmose III. In his report about the work in Aswan, Senenmut refers to Hatshepsut as "the one to whom Ra has actually given the kingship." It was the first step toward claiming the crown for Hatshepsut. If Hatshepsut were not just a regent, but the king, she wouldn't have to give up power when Thutmose III grew up.

"Pharaoh's workers" by Fortunino Matania

Soon images on the walls of temples and tombs started showing Hatshepsut playing the role of a pharaoh – standing directly in front of gods, wearing kingly headgear and performing rituals only pharaohs were allowed to perform. Then, at a big religious festival in Thebes, the oracle of Amun announced that gods had chosen Hatshepsut to be king. Not queen, but king! It was certainly bizarre, but nobody dared to speak their mind – Hatshepsut's star was rising.

Next, at the same festival, the two obelisks cut for Thutmose III, were unveiled. Instead of Thutmose's name, however, the obelisks were carved with the name of Hatshepsut and her images as 'king'! Thutmose III was around 8 years old, and Hatshepsut was around 30 when she was crowned. In inscriptions at the Karnak Temple of Amun, Hatshepsut claimed that Amun placed the crown on her head with his own hand. She also announced that Thutmose I was not really her father, her real father was god Amun himself. Some earlier temple reliefs showing Hatshepsut and Thutmose III as co-rulers, have the image of the child-king partially erased – probably on the order of Hatshepsut.

Despite the success of her power grab, Hatshepsut's position was still weak. A woman, she had claimed a man's role. She figured she could fix that problem by pretending she was actually a man. In her first images as 'king,' Hatshepsut wore a dress, the shape of her body was soft and feminine. However she was shown with a man's hairstyle and headgear – a short wig and a crown with ram's horns. By the time Thutmose III turned 13, Hatshepsut's statues showed her with a beard and an upper body of a man, although her face remained feminine. Even later into Hatshepsut's reign, her statues evolved to present her as a man, even making her face masculine, with a square jaw.

Left: the Temple of Hatshepsut in Thebes
Right: Thutmose III (left) and Hatshepsut (right) from a temple in Karnak

Hatshepsut built herself a temple – the Temple of Millions of Years – where we find the following inscription: "He who will praise Hatshepsut, will live. He who will speak an evil thing, ignoring her majesty, will die." Clearly the opposition to Hatshepsut's 'kingship' was growing. Thutmose III was already 14, and Hatshepsut's enemies started gathering behind him.

Hatshepsut's reign was mostly peaceful, although she did wage a war against Nubia, and even personally led her army into battle! She built many temples and monuments – some of the most brilliant creations of Egyptian architecture. She established a trading route to the Land of Punt, an ancient kingdom rich in gold, ebony, and ivory, located probably south of Egypt.

On the other hand, Hatshepsut was clearly perceived as a weak ruler by foreign kings. The lands conquered by Hatshepsut's ancestors stopped paying tribute to Egypt, and Hatshepsut's government couldn't restore order. The Egyptian empire was falling apart. At home Hatshepsut's officials were also taking advantage of her weakness. Her favorite architect Sen-Mut smuggled images of himself into Hatshepsut's temples, placing them in such a way that they were hidden behind open doors!

When Thutmose III turned 18 years old, Hatshepsut couldn't keep him in the shadows any longer. He became the head of the Egyptian army. Temple images from that period show Hatshepsut and Thutmose – looking like two brothers – walking in sacred processions together, although Hatshepsut walks first, and Thutmose follows her. But even this continuing 'propaganda' of Hatshepsut's royal power didn't save her from being pushed aside.

Above: Hatshepsut portrayed as king and Thutmose III portrayed as a sphinx; Right: ancient Egyptian game "Hounds and Jackals"

Above: "Worship in the tempe of Sobek, the crocodile-headed god of the Nile"; Right: "Pharaoh's Hall of State"

Egyptologists suggested that Hatshepsut's plan was to make her daughter, Nefrure, the next 'king' of Egypt, but Thutmose III won. In the Temple of Millions of Years they found a relief of a woman likely to be Nefrure. She is portrayed with the attributes of royal power, and her size is enormous in comparison to the images that surround her. The relief was clearly re-carved later to remove the features of a 'king.' The inscription with the name was erased and replaced with the name of Hatshepsut's mother.

Hatshepsut died when Thutmose III was 22. He immediately had Hatshesut's name erased from many of her statues, and, since she was mostly portrayed as a man, the statues were inscribed with the names of his father and grandfather. 25 years later, when Thutmose selected his son Amenhotep II as his heir and future pharaoh, he decided to erase any traces of Hatshepsut, to make sure that nothing of that nature happened to his son. Most statues of Hatshepsut were broken and destroyed, and her images on temple walls turned into Thutmose I and Thutmose II.

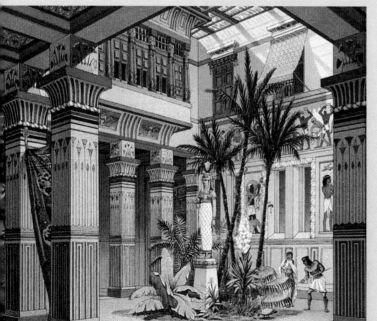

Left: "Courtyard of an Egyptian palace"

Below: Egyptian collar, gold on wood, 1981-1802 BC

PHARAOH THUTMOSE III

REIGNED 1479 – 1425 BC

During the roughly 20 years of Hatshepsut's reign, Thutmose III received education and military training preparing him for his future role as the pharaoh. We don't know how Hatshepsut died. What we do know is that Thutmose claimed the throne. Most likely Hatshepsut died soon after. She was buried with royal honors. Once Hatshepsut was dead, Thutmose started erasing her image from temple reliefs and paintings – sometimes turning her figure into the images of his father and grandfather, and sometimes even replacing her with abnormally large plates of offerings.

Thutmose III is often called the greatest pharaoh in the history of Egypt and 'the Napoleon of Egypt.' Just like France under Napoleon, the Egyptian empire expanded its borders and reached the height of its power during the reign of Thutmose III. Thutmose III fought 16 wars over the course of 20 years, capturing around 350 cities. He is said to have never lost a battle!

At the beginning of Thutmose's reign the Eastern provinces of the Egyptian empire rebelled.

"Pharaoh marching to war" by Heinrich Leutemann

Those were the provinces that had stopped obeying Egyptian rule under Hatshepsut. Thutmose led his army into the territories of present-day Israel and Syria, defeated the rebels there and pushed the border of Egypt as far east as the River Euphrates.

Thutmose constructed huge obelisks to commemorate his successes and victories, but none of them still stands in Egypt. When the Romans discovered two of these obelisks in 12 BC, they were lying buried in the sand. The Romans took the obelisks to Alexandria and placed them by the entrance of a temple dedicated to Julius Caesar. Because the temple had been built by Cleopatra, the obelisks became known as "Cleopatra's Needles." In the 19th century, the Egyptian government gave one obelisk to England. The second obelisk was given to the United States by the Turkish ruler of Egypt, Ismail Pasha, in honor of the opening of the Suez Canal. It was installed in New York City, in Central Park, next to the Metropolitan Museum of Art, where it stands to this day.

There are a number of ancient documents describing the military campaigns of Thutmose III. One of these campaigns defeated a rebellion in the Levantine city of Megiddo, also known under its Greek name, Armageddon. The Canaanite Prince of Kadesh had gathered a coalition of city-states and raised an army that occupied the Megiddo Pass – a passage through a mountain ridge that overlooks a valley.

Right: gold sandals of the queen of Thutmose III
Below: Cleopatra's Needle in Alexandria, and
Cleopatra's needles in London (left)
and New York (right)

Canaanite princes arrived at Megiddo Pass in chariots of gold and silver, say ancient chronicles. They camped in beautiful tents, filled with carved and decorated furniture. When the army of Thutmose III drew near, his generals advised him against entering the narrow Megiddo Pass, where the Egyptian soldiers would have to walk in single file – one behind another.

But Thutmose didn't want the enemy to think: "Has his majesty set out on another road because he has become afraid of us?" Instead he rode at the head of his army in a golden chariot, carrying an image of the god Amon-Ra, who, he told his generals, had promised victory. Indeed, the Canaanites did not expect Thutmose to take the Megiddo Pass. They camped at its Northern end and did nothing as the army of Thutmose walked in a single file, following the pharaoh, for an entire day.

Finally when the Egyptians attacked, the Canaanites broke ranks and fled, leaving behind over a thousand chariots and their rich camp. In the town of Megiddo, people had so little faith in their own army, that they had locked the city gates expecting the enemy any moment. The fleeing army ended up trapped by the closed Megiddo gates, defenseless. Some citizens made ropes from their clothes and lifted the panic-stricken warriors up onto the walls. The Egyptians laid siege to the city.

After seven months' siege the Canaanites sent out their children carrying weapons to offer them to the pharaoh as a sign of surrender.

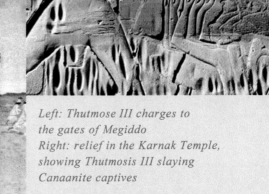

Left: Thutmose III charges to the gates of Megiddo
Right: relief in the Karnak Temple, showing Thutmosis III slaying Canaanite captives

The surviving city defenders were standing on their walls begging the pharaoh for forgiveness. Thutmose generously forgave them on the condition that they swear to be loyal to Egypt for their lifetime. The Canaanites went home to their villages on donkeys, since the peace agreement gave all their horses to the Egyptians!

Running the imperial provinces of Egypt, Thutmose III invented a new way to ensure the loyalty of local kings and princes. He made them send their kids as hostages to Egypt. While the young princes lived at his court, they were educated in Egyptian values and eventually felt more at home in the Egyptian capital than in their native lands. When they returned to their hometowns and became kings, it was guaranteed they would be good friends of Egypt. This method of educating future provincial rulers in the imperial centers of the world has continued to today.

Thutmose III was passionate about hunting, sports, and martial arts. Tomb and temple inscriptions of his era tell us how the pharaoh hunted and killed 120 elephants in northern Syria, how he killed 7 lions and captured 12 wild bulls within an hour, and drove an arrow nearly 9 inches through a 2-inch-thick target.

Discovery of a tomb that was robbed;
an alabaster jar with the name of Thutmose III

PHARAOH AKHENATEN

REIGNED AROUND 1353-1336 BC

Akhenaten, or Amenhotep IV, was the son of Amenhotep III and the grandson of Thutmose III.

His mother was a foreigner, and not of royal origin, which prevented him from any lawful claim to the throne. But his brother, the crown prince, died, and Amenhotep IV was selected by the oracle to be the next pharaoh. When he was around 30 years old, he finally became king. During his reign Egypt was at the top of its wealth and power. There were no military threats. The kings of the Levant and Syria were paying tribute, Nubia and Kush in present-day Sudan were sending a steady trickle of gold to the royal treasury of Egypt and loads of granite for the pharaoh's building projects. As tradition required, Amenhotep had a number of wives, and in the 4th year of his reign he selected one of them, Nefertiti, whose name means 'the beautiful one has come,' as the Great Royal Wife.

It's likely that early in his reign Amenhotep IV faced opposition from the priests and elite families who had never truly accepted him as their lawful king. That put him on a path of rebellion against custom and tradition. Unlike pharaohs before him, he turned away from the cult of Amun and started paying more and more attention to Egypt's sun god Aten. It's possible that his mother's foreign family worshipped only one god, the god of light – Aten – and rejected all other Egyptian gods. As a result Amun's priests – an enormously wealthy and powerful group of families – hated Amenhotep, who was firmly on his way toward undermining their influence and sources of wealth.

On the surface, life in Thebes, the Egyptian capital, went as before. The king and his court participated in endless parades, temple processions, and rituals. But a new movement known as the "Amarna Revolution" was underway.

the "Eye of Horus" amulet, Egypt, 332-330 BC

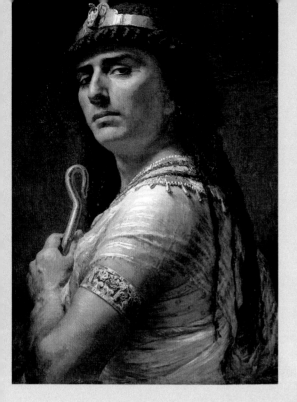

The priests of Amun pushed for the expansion of the empire, for conquests to enrich their temple. But Amenhotep didn't care much for military glory or plundered treasures. His new court consisted of men who rose to high positions from families of no importance. The members of the noble and priestly families were losing their offices, privileges, and sources of income.

Nefertiti, the Great Royal Wife, was now always by the king's side – in real life and on the walls of the temples and monuments where her image was given visibility that no queen had ever enjoyed before. The portraits of the royal family included scenes unheard of in the art of Ancient Egypt – the king and queen kissing, playing with their kids, eating, receiving guests, or riding a chariot together. In addition Nefertiti was shown fighting the enemy armies – something that had never been done before. Never before had crowds gathered in front of the royal palace to catch gold trinkets thrown by the pharaoh and his wife from the window. Until then the pharaohs had made few public appearances and nobody had ever seen their families. Amenhotep IV insisted that in his statues and paintings he should be portrayed in a particular way – with a strangely long face, slanty narrow eyes, stick-thin arms and legs, tentacle-like curved fingers, and disproportionately large belly and hips.

Above: "An Egyptian priest" by Frederick Arthur Bridgman
Right: Akhenaten

Did he really look like this, or did he just want to look different as an act of rebellion? The colossal statues of Amenhotep IV at Karnak temple show these characteristics in such an exaggerated form as to almost look like caricatures.

Soon the king dumped his name, Amenhotep – which means 'Amun is satisfied' – and took a new name, Akhenaten, which means 'the one who is beneficial to the Aten.' To draw the line between the worship of Amun – 'the Hidden One' – and Aten, the Sun disk, Akhenaten made his whole court and all the priests stand in the blazing sun for hours making offerings to the sun as it traveled across the sky. The dark cool chambers deep inside massive Amun temples were no longer appropriate places of worship. The Aten temples at Karnak consisted almost entirely of vast open-air courts, with no interior space at all. In The Amarna letters – the correspondence between the Egyptian government and the rulers of its provinces – foreign diplomats complained bitterly about the endless festivals and rituals in the sun without any attempt to provide shade.

In the 5th year of his reign Akhenaten moved his court and government out of Heliopolis, Memphis, and Thebes, and founded a new capital in Middle Egypt – Akhetaten, the 'Horizon of the Aten' (modern Amarna). The town was richly adorned with monuments. In a very short period of time Akhenaten built a lot of gigantic temples and palaces.

Akhenaten and Nefertiti had 6 daughters, but no sons. However, Akhenaten had sons with his other wives. Nefertiti knew that once a crown prince was selected she would have to share power with the crown prince's mother.

"Divination (fortune-telling) using a jackal at the temple of the jackal-headed god Anubis"

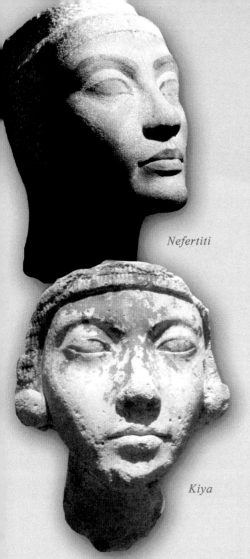

Nefertiti

Kiya

It's likely that Nefertiti worked constantly to get rid of potential rivals. Kiya, one of Akhenaten's other wives, became the target of Nefertiti's anger. In the inscriptions that mention Kiya, her name was erased and replaced with the names of Nefertiti's daughters.

Around the 12th year of Akhenaten's reign, Nefertiti suddenly disappeared from documents and inscriptions as the Great Royal Wife. At the same time there appeared a new co-ruler named Smenkhkare. Most historians agree that the co-ruler was Nefertiti who was preparing to become 'king' after Akhenaten's death. As king she could hold on to power – just like Hatshepsut – even though the crown prince was not her son.

In the following years, three of Akhenaten and Nefertiti's daughters died of plague. Egypt also suffered a serious military defeat, losing Northern Syria. The *Amarna Letters,* written in the Akkadian language on clay tablets, contain desperate requests for the pharaoh's help from Egyptian provinces that could no longer hold out against Egypt's enemies.

To keep the momentum of his reforms going, Akhenaten started a campaign against polytheism – worship of many gods. He ordered the names of the god Amun and his wife Mut be erased from the monuments of his royal ancestors, even those written high up on the obelisks, many stories above the ground!

Nefertiti's chariot

Next he shut down temples of Amun and other gods and ordered any amulet worn around one's neck or in a pocket to be destroyed if it had the name of any god other than the god of the Sun. Even the plural form of 'god' – 'gods' – was erased from the walls of tombs and temples.

Then, to the horror of Egyptians, a total eclipse of the Sun occurred in 1338 BC, turning day into night for 5 minutes and 48 seconds. Egyptians did not know how to predict solar eclipses. People were terrified. Maybe it was because of the eclipse that Akhenaten's reforms slowed down toward the end of his reign.

When Akhenaten died at age 50 in the 17th year of his reign, his wife and 'co-king' Nefertiti was still in her 20s and his heir – son or nephew – Tutankhaten, the future Pharaoh Tutankhamun, or 'King Tut' – was 6 years old.

"Temple of Isis at Philae" by David Roberts

In 1907 in the Valley of the Kings, archaeologists found a tomb known as "KV 55," right by the tomb of Tutankhamun. Genetic analysis suggested that the mummy in that tomb was the son of Amenhotep III and King Tut's father. The tomb was undecorated and unmarked, but a few bricks found inside were engraved with magic spells that included Akhenaten's name. The tomb also contained he remains of Kiya. Based on that, some archaeologists believe that the mummy is Akhenaten.

Relief of Queen Nefertiti

PHARAOH TUTANKHAMUN

REIGNED 1332 – 1323 BC

After the death of Akhenaten, King Smenkhkare – who, most historians believe was actually Nefertiti – became the pharaoh of Egypt. Smenkhkare selected Nefertiti's daughter Meritaten to be his Great Royal Wife. In the tomb of Meryre II in Amarna there is a drawing that shows Smenkhkare wearing a man's kilt, but with a woman's garment around his chest! Nefertiti died a few years into her reign as Pharaoh Smenkhkare, and Akhenaten's son (or nephew) Tutankhaten became king.

In no time Tutankhaten changed his name to Tutankhamun – 'the living image of Amun,' and restored the worship of Amun. His Great Royal Wife, Nefirtiti's daughter Ankhesenpaaten ('She lives for the Aten'), changed her name to Ankhesenamun ('Her life is of Amun').

The opposition to Akhenaten's reforms had grown so powerful that it was impossible to keep the *status quo* (Latin: *status quo* = things as they are). An inscription in Tutankhamun's tomb lists the consequences of Akhenaten's reforms: "The temples of the gods and goddesses had gone to pieces. Their shrines had become desolate and had become overgrown mounds... The land was topsy-turvy, and the gods turned their backs upon this land. When people prayed to a god to seek counsel from him, he would never come at all."

Right: King Tut's pendant
Left: King Tut's tomb

Tutankhamun's vizirs and advisors – including one of his generals, Horemheb, who would become the next pharaoh – encouraged anew the worship of Egyptian gods, restored the sacred shrines of Amun, restored the privileges of the priestly elite, and ordered the artisans and architects to bring back traditional Egyptian art. The Amarna revolution was over! A counterrevolution began.

Newcomers at the royal court who had gained government jobs and wealth through their loyalty to Akhenaten were thrown out. Tutankhamun "appointed priests from the children of the old noble families. Each was the son of a known man, whose name was well-known." The temples were paid damages: "All the property of the temples was doubled, tripled, and quadrupled in silver, gold, lapis lazuli, and turquoise..." The pharaoh donated money from his own budget to increase the number of priests and their staff at the temples. This was a total surrender. The pharaoh was, once again, the hostage of the ruling elite.

The royal court and the government moved from Amarna to Memphis. As archaeologists explored the site of Tell el Amarna – the location of Akhenaten's capital – they noticed that the doors of temples and palaces were neatly sealed with bricks. It looked like the inhabitants of the city left with the intention of coming back one day. But that day never came.

Tutankhamun – or King Tut – reigned for 9 years until he died of malaria at 18. Tutankhamun had no kids. After his death, his chief advisors Ay and Horemheb fought for the throne. Ay became king and proposed marriage to Tutankhamun's Great Royal Wife Ankhesenamun, even though she despised him for being of non-royal origin.

"An Egyptian by the door of his house"
by Lawrence Alma-Tadema

Archaeologists found a letter sent by Ankhesenamun to the Hittite king. "My husband died," says the letter. "And I don't have a son. But they say you have many sons. If you could send one of your sons here, he would become my husband. I will never choose a husband from one of my servants." The Hittite prince sent to marry Ankhesenamun was murdered on the way, and Ankhesenamun most likely had to marry Ay. A ring dating to this period shows the names of Ay and Ankhesenamun inscribed together, indicating they were a couple.

Ay's reign was short – only about four years. After that, power passed to Horemheb, the commander of the Egyptian army. His first act as pharaoh was to shut down the temples of the Aten built by Akhenaten. He also carved his name over the names of Tutankhamun and Ay on their monuments. The names of Akhenaten, Tutankhamun and Ay were erased from the official lists of the Egyptian kings.

Akhenaten's radical reforms had thrown Egypt into chaos. Horemheb's 30-year rule fully restored tradition inside Egypt and claimed back its international prestige. Another military man, the general Ramses, served as Horemheb's vizier and after Horemheb's death he became Pharaoh Ramses I, the founder of the new, 19th dynasty (1292–1190 BC).

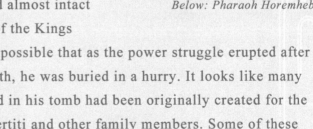

Above: a princess from the family of Akhenaten and Pharaoh Ay
Below: Pharaoh Horemheb

In 1922 King Tut's tomb was discovered almost intact in the Valley of the Kings in Thebes. It's possible that as the power struggle erupted after King Tut's death, he was buried in a hurry. It looks like many treasures found in his tomb had been originally created for the burials of Nefertiti and other family members. Some of these precious objects have someone else's names erased and Tutankhamun's name written on top.

Also, King Tut's gold mask has pierced ears, but Tutankhamun did not wear earrings. The face of the mask is made from gold of a different quality than the rest of the mask, and there is a welding line around it.

King Tut's mummy lay inside three nested coffins placed in the stone sarcophagus. The innermost coffin was of solid gold. The two outer coffins were made of wood with gold leaf hammered over it. The mummy wrappings were filled with gold jewelry and amulets. The rooms of the tomb were overflowing with furniture, statues, Tutankhamun's clothes, weapons, and chariots.

The crook and flail in the hands of King Tut's image on the coffin lid were symbols of pharaonic authority. A crook is a shepherd's cane with a hooked handle. A flail is a rod with three beaded strands of leather – a shepherd's whip.

Above: King Tut's gold mask
Below left: "King Tut on a boat" by Peter Jackson
Below right: Howard Carter opens King Tut's coffin, and the furniture inside King Tut's tomb

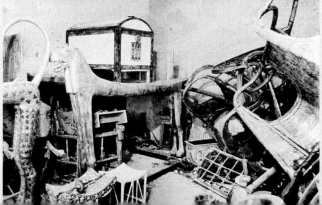

The discovery of King Tut's tomb gave rise to the legend of the pharaoh's curse. Soon after the tomb was opened, a few mysterious events occurred. A cobra supposedly killed the pet canary belonging to Howard Carter, the explorer who discovered King Tut's tomb and was the first person to enter it. Next, Lord Carnarvon, who funded the archeological dig of King Tut's tomb, died from a mosquito bite. At the exact moment of his death – says the legend – his dog howled and dropped dead, and all the lights in Cairo suddenly went out.

"It's the curse that targets anyone who enters the tomb," announced the media.

More and more stories about mysterious deaths appeared. It's entirely possible that entering the tomb made some people sick – but it wasn't the curse, it was the harmful bacteria later discovered growing in the tomb.

Right: a gold ram head amulet, Egypt, 712-664 BC
Below: "An Egyptian widow by the coffin of her husband"
by Lawrence Alma-Tadema

PHARAOH RAMSES II

REIGNED 1279–1213 BC

Ramses II, third king of the 19th dynasty, was named
crown prince at the age of 14. He ruled for 60 years and
died at the age of 80.

Ramses' father, Seti I, started training Ramses for
kingship very early. At age 10, Ramses was already
advanced in military arts and ranked as a captain
in his father's army. Once he was appointed a crown
prince, he was given his own palace, a household
he had to manage, and accompanied his father on
all his military campaigns.

Historians of ancient Greece and Rome recorded many legends about an Egyptian king
they called Sesostris. Scholars believe that these legends came from different eras of
Egyptian history, and that some of them echo the biographical facts of Ramses II.

Here is a legend we find in the *Bibliotheca Historica – The Library of History* by
Diodorus Siculus: "When Sesostris was born, his father did a thing worthy of a great
man and a king. He gathered from all over Egypt boys who were born on the same day,

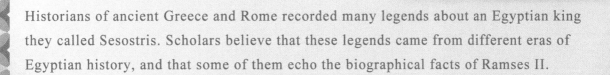

hired for them guardians and tutors, and raised them together with his son. He figured out that children who grow up together would be most loyal to one another as fellow fighters in wars. He paid for their education and military training, and none of them was ever allowed to have anything to eat unless he had first run one hundred and eighty stades."

Ramses II defeats the Nubians

Ramses II was successful in wars, but he is most remembered for his extensive building programs and for the numerous colossal statues of him found all over Egypt. Diodorus Siculus also describes a monument of Ramses II, using his Greek name, Ozymandyas. "Ten stades from the tombs... stands a monument of the king known as Ozymandias... beside the entrance are three statues, each of a single block of black stone, of which one, that is seated, is the largest statue in Egypt. And it is not merely for its size that this work is worthy of praise, but it is also marvellous in its artistic quality and excellent because of the nature of the stone, since in that whole huge block there is not a single crack or blemish to be seen. The inscription on the statue says: 'King of Kings am I, Ozymandias. If anyone would know how great I am and where I lie, let him try to outdo me in his works.'"

'People of Israel in Egypt' by Edward John Poynter

In 1817 the British Museum acquired the fragment of a statue of Ramses II. The British public was so excited to see the statue that, ahead of its arrival in London, the great English poet Percy Bysshe Shelley wrote his famous sonnet *Ozymandias*:

The colossi (giant statues) of Ramses II

I met a traveller from an antique land
Who said: "Two vast and trunkless legs of stone
Stand in the desert. Near them, on the sand,
Half sunk, a shattered visage lies, whose frown,
And wrinkled lip, and sneer of cold command,
Tell that its sculptor well those passions read
Which yet survive, stamped on these lifeless things,
The hand that mocked them and the heart that fed:
And on the pedestal these words appear:
'My name is Ozymandias, king of kings:
Look at my works, ye Mighty, and despair!'
Nothing beside remains. Round the decay
Of that colossal wreck, boundless and bare
The lone and level sands stretch far away."

Here is another Sesostris legend that sounds like it's really about Ramses II. It has come down to us through the books of Diodorus Siculus: "When Sesostris conquered foreign kingdoms, he allowed the local kings to rule over the people as before, but at specified times they had to come to Egypt bringing him gifts. Sesostris welcomed them and showed them honor, but whenever he intended to visit a temple or city he would remove the horses from his four-horse chariot and make the kings pull it. This way he showed to all men, that having conquered the mightiest of kings, he had no one who could compete with him for the prize of excellence."

Ramses II built and remodeled hundreds of temples, tombs, and palaces, turning Egypt into one giant construction site. His architects and sculptors couldn't keep up with his building enthusiasm. Fortunately there was a way to create new monuments without much effort: Hundreds of statues of pharaohs from the previous dynasties were 'modified,' with the pharaoh's name erased and replaced with the name of Ramses II. In the Egyptian village of Abu Simbel in Aswan, there is a temple with four statues of gods sitting side-by-side, including Ramses. Wall reliefs show the pharaoh making offerings to... himself as a god!

Both contemporaries of Ramses II and the following generations of Egyptians viewed him as one of the greatest pharaohs. Nine pharaohs following him took his name – from Ramses III to Ramses XI.

Starting around 1200 BC – toward the end of the Bronze Age – the so-called *Sea Peoples* started migrating to the Mediterranean region from somewhere in Central Europe or Asia Minor. These Sea Peoples included the Philistines, some Aegean tribes, and many other groups. This was the beginning of the 'Bronze Age collapse' – the difficult transition to the Iron Age that destroyed or weakened a number of civilizations around the Mediterranean Sea. One of the first recorded clashes between Egyptians and the Sea Peoples happened during the reign of Ramses II.

In the 5th year of his reign, Ramses led his army to take the fortress of Kadesh in present-day Syria. Having crossed Palestine and Lebanon, Ramses sent a special task force to take the seaport of Simyra and kept marching toward Kadesh. Ramses captured Hittite spies, but the spies gave him false information about the location of the Hittite army. Thinking that Kadesh was unprotected, Ramses led his troops to the walls of the city only to discover that the whole Hittite army – 2,500 chariots, with three men to a chariot – was hiding on the other side of the city.

The Hittites attacked. The Egyptian army broke ranks and fled in disorder. Ramses and a small unit of his guards were surrounded by the enemy and fought for their lives. Fortunately, the Simyra task force appeared just in time to prevent the disaster. Leaving Kadesh behind, the Egyptians went home.

The Battle of Kadesh has an important place in Egyptian history. While most descriptions of battles carved on Egyptian monuments simply praise the pharaoh and the god that 'ensured' Egyptian victory, the account of the Battle of Kadesh carved on temple walls in Egypt and Nubia provides a detailed description of real events.

Of course, Ramses II is portrayed in the Egyptian accounts of the battle as the winner. The stone carving shows panic-stricken Hittites throwing themselves into the river and bears an inscription: "The King charged into the midst of the enemy, while he was alone by himself... He slaughtered them... overthrew them into the waters of the Orontes. His majesty was behind them like a fierce-eyed lion".

a silver Egyptian wine cup from the era of Ramses II

According to a legend, the Hittites had 'war lions' in their army! Above: "Ramses II fights against the war lions of the Hittites" by Carl Oderich (painting) and Heinrich Lautemann (print); "Hittite prisoners before Ramses II" by Heinrich Lauteman

Ironically, the Hittite King Muwattali II also claimed victory! A Hittite relief explaining The Battle of Kadesh is accompanied by the following statement: "King Muwattalli and the King of Egypt battled with each other over the Amurru (Kadesh). Muwattalli defeated the king of Egypt and destroyed the Land of Amurru with his weapons and subjugated it."

When Jean Francois Champollion deciphered the ancient Egyptian language, the first Egyptian word he read was Ramses. Scholars had already read the names of Greek rulers written in hieroglyphic writing - Alexander, Ptolemy, and Cleopatra, but they couldn't read Egyptian names that had no Greek equivalents. Champollion used his knowledge of the Coptic language as he tried to read a hieroglyphic inscription from the temple at Abu Simbel. Coptic is an ancient language still used in Egyptian Christian communities.

Champollion focused on the word ⊙𓏥𓈖𓈖. He knew that 𓈖 was likely an S. ⊙ was the hieroglyph for the Sun. In Coptic, the sun is Ra. The hieroglyph 𓏥 was translated as 'to give birth' on the Rosetta Stone. In Coptic, to give birth is 'mise'. So Champollion read ⊙𓏥𓈖𓈖 as Ra – M – S – S. Ramses? To verify his guess Champollion read 𓇓𓏥𓈖 as Thot – M – S, Thutmose!

The average lifespan in Ancient Egypt was 40-45 years for men and 30-35 for women. So when Ramses II died at the age of 80, his 12 eldest sons had already died of old age! His 13th son, Merneptah, was appointed the crown prince, and he wasn't young either. The mummy of Ramses II is now in the Egyptian Museum in Cairo.

Below: Ramses II victory relief; Right: The Rosetta Stone

EGYPT AND THE BIBLE

Along with its sacred content, the Old Testament of the Bible contains ancient chronicles and documents related to the history of Ancient Israel. It also describes some events that happened in Ancient Egypt and mentions a few Egyptian pharaohs. However, scholars have not been able to synchronize (put side-by-side on the timeline) the events described in the Bible and the events known from Egyptian documents and chronicles. Egyptian sources and the Bible use different types of chronology (order and the dating of events), and the names of Egyptian and Israeli historical figures sounded different in the Egyptian and Hebrew languages.

The biblical *Book of Genesis* says that Joseph, the youngest son of the Old Testament patriarch Jacob, was sold into slavery and ended up in Egypt (Genesis 37-50). A talented and hard-working man, he eventually became a vizier of the Egyptian pharaoh, and invited his father and 11 brothers to settle in Egypt, in the Land of Goshen (the eastern Nile Delta). Which Egyptian pharaoh hired Joseph as his vizier? Scholars have not been able to answer this question. As a result, many of them treat the story of Joseph as a legend, a symbolic narrative, rather than an actual historical event.

The biblical *Book of Exodus* says that the descendants of Jacob's sons, the people of Israel, lived in Egypt until a new pharaoh forced them to work as slaves on his construction projects.

"Joseph – the vizier" by Lawrence Alma-Tadema

The pharaoh also ordered that all newborn boys in Israeli families should be killed in order to reduce the growth of the Israeli population. The Israelis rebelled and, led by Moses, left Egypt in the event known as the *Exodus*. The pharaoh chased them with his army, but his army drowned in the Red Sea. Which Egyptian pharaoh was the pharaoh of the Exodus?

Most ancient authors and church fathers believed that the actual historical basis of the Exodus was the conquest of Egypt by the Hyksos and their departure from Egypt 100 years later. This is supported by the fact that the Hyksos were from the region of present-day Israel and spoke a Semitic language related to Hebrew. Ancient scholars identified Ahmose I (Amasis I), the Egyptian ruler who drove the Hyksos out of the Nile Delta, as the pharaoh of Exodus. Some scholars name Dedumose II who ruled Egypt as the Hyksos invasion began, or Thutmose I and his queen Hatshepsut who ruled immediately after the defeat of the Hyksos, as possible candidates for the pharaoh from the book of Exodus.

Yet other scholars believe that the pharaoh of Exodus was Ramses II because the biblical books of *Genesis* and *Exodus* mention a place name – a town named Rameses – which is also mentioned in an inscription on a monument created during the reign of Ramses II. Popular movies about *Exodus* portray Ramses II as the pharaoh defeated by Moses and the people of Israel.

Above left: "Exodus"
by Horace William Petherick
Above: "Let my people go! – Moses
speaks to the pharaoh"
by James Tissot
Left: "Exodus" by Anton Robert Leinweber

PSAMTIK I

REIGNED 664–610 BC

In the 9th and 8th centuries BC Egypt split into two states – Upper Egypt and Lower Egypt – and was engulfed in a civil war waged by rival pharaohs. As a result, large portions of Egypt fell into the hands of the Assyrian empire.

The Nubians – the native people of Upper Egypt and the region of present-day Sudan – took advantage of that. The Nubian Kingdom of Kush invaded Egypt in 732 BC. Nubian warlords – often called the Black Pharaohs – ruled the portions of Egypt that were not occupied by the Assyrians for about 100 years, until the Assyrians drove them out.

In 671 BC the Assyrian king Esarhaddon crossed the Sinai Desert, invaded Egypt, and destroyed the Kingdom of Kush. Assyrian documents quote King Esarhaddon saying: "All Nubians I deported from Egypt, leaving not one to do homage to me." Instead of Nubians he appointed native Egyptian princes to rule over different parts of Egypt. In 656 BC Psamtik, one of these native princes, hired Greek mercenaries, revolted against the Assyrians, united Egypt, and freed it from Assyrian control. Psamtik I started a new dynasty – the last native

Assyrian soldiers with Nubian prisoners – relief from Nineveh, modern-day Iraq

Egyptian dynasty before Egypt was conquered by the Persians, and then later fell into the hands of Alexander the Great.

The highest-ranking priestess of the Amun cult in Ancient Egypt had the title God's Wife of Amun. When Psamtik took control of Egypt, the God's Wife of Amun was the daughter of the last Nubian pharaoh. Instead of removing her by force Psamtik made her adopt his own daughter as her heiress and the next high priestess. This created the impression of the peaceful handover of power from the Nubian priesthood to Psamtik. Strategic moves like this made Psamtik both a feared and a popular ruler.

Herodotus recorded a legend of how Psamtik I came to power. Psamtik and 11 other Egyptian princes came to a temple to offer sacrifices. "The high priest brought out the golden cups which they commonly used for libations" writes Herodotus. A 'libation' is a drink ritually poured out on the ground or on an altar as an offering to a god. However, the high priest miscalculated and gave the princes 11 cups instead of 12. "Psamtik was the last in line and he received no cup. So he took off his bronze helmet, held it out, and poured the libation with it... Then the other princes remembered the oracle saying that whoever should pour libation from a vessel of bronze would rule over the whole of Egypt."

"Psamtik's Libation"
Below: Assyrian warrior costumes

The princes felt threatened and chased Psamtik away into the marshes of the Nile Delta. Psamtik was outraged that they had dealt with him so unjustly and set his mind on revenge. He sent a messenger to the Oracle of Leto in the town of Buto. The oracle said that Psamtik would have a chance at revenge when he saw men of bronze coming from the sea. Psamtik secretly disbelieved the oracle, but suddenly a group of Greek pirates were forced by a storm to the coast of Egypt. They had armor made of bronze.

Egyptian warriors did not wear body armor. Hearing about the foreigners in bronze armor, Psamtik saw in this the fulfilment of the oracle. He made friends with the Greeks, and promised them great rewards if they would join him. With their help he defeated the eleven princes and became the master of Egypt. According to Herodotus, Psamtik gave the Greeks land and riches, and "sent Egyptian boys to the Greek's camp to study the Greek language. These boys became the ancestors of the Egyptian interpreters." In his version of this legend Diodorus Siculus adds that Psamtik "gave his sons a Greek education."

Herodotus also recorded a legend describing the first ever psychological experiment. It was conducted during the reign of Psamtik I. Psamtik wanted to know whether people were born with an ability to speak this or that language or whether they learned it as children. He ordered a shepherd to raise two babies in a remote place. The shepherd was not allowed to talk to the babies. When the kids turned two, one of them suddenly said the word that sounded like βεκός – 'bekos' – the Phrygian word for bread. Psamtik concluded that people were born with knowledge of the Phrygian language, so therefore it must be the original language of all mankind. Phrygian, an Indo-European language related to Greek, was spoken in ancient times in Anatolia, or Asia Minor.

At the Heliopolis site in Cairo, archaeologists found a *colossus* of Psamtik I. It was broken and submerged in groundwater.
Colossus (plural: *colossi*) is an oversized, huge statue (from Greek *kolossos* – gigantic statue). Cut from solid quartzite, the statue had been intentionally destroyed in ancient times. First it was heated on fire and then splashed with cold water to force the stone to crack.

Bronze Greek armor, 4th century BC – a muscle cuirass (body armor) and a helmet

Left: Excavation of the Psamtik colossus

AMASIS II

REIGNED 570-526 BC

Amasis (or Ahmose) II was the last Egyptian pharaoh before Egypt fell under the rule of the Persian Empire. Almost all we know about him come from Herodotus' *History*.

Amasis was not of royal origin, he was a military commander under the Pharaoh Apries. At some point the pharaoh sent him to suppress a revolt occurring among Egyptian soldiers. The rebels belonged to an Egyptian division sent by Apries to Cyrene in Libya on a mission that had ended in a disaster. The soldiers suspected that they had been sent to their death because the pharaoh was afraid of the growing power of his army and wanted to replace them with the Greek mercenaries. When Amasis reached out to the rebels to negotiate, they proclaimed him king! "So Amasis went to the rebels," writes Herodotus, "but as he spoke with them, persuading them, a certain man came behind him and put a helmet on his head, crying out that he had crowned him king."

The rest of the native Egyptian army joined Amasis. A battle took place, and the Egyptians defeated the Greek mercenaries. Apries "was taken alive and brought to the city of Saïs, to his own house, which was now the palace of King Amasis. And for a while Amasis kept him in the palace, treating him with all honor. But when the Egyptians murmured against him, saying that he did wrong having such respect to one that was his enemy and the enemy of the people, then the King gave up Apries to the Egyptians, and they strangled him."

"So Amasis reigned over the land of Egypt," Herodotus continues, "and at first the Egyptians despised him because he had been one of them, and because his family was not known in the land. But he won his people, not by forcing them to like him, but by his cleverness. He was very rich. In his house he had a footbath of gold, in which he and his guests washed their feet before feasts. He took this vessel of gold, melted it, and made from it an image of a god. And all the Egyptians admired and worshipped it. Then King Amasis addressed them, saying, 'See, this image was a footbath used to wash off dirt, but now you worship it. Know that I am like this gold. Before, I was one of you, but now I am your king. Therefore must you do me such honor as is appropriate for a king.' In this manner he made the Egyptians serve him willingly."

Herodotus collected quite a few historical *anecdotes* – entertaining stories – about Pharaoh Amasis. "His manner of life was this," he writes. "Amasis would rise very early in the morning, and would do the business of his kingdom with much zeal until the time when the market-place begins to fill, which is before noon. But after this he would drink and chat with all sorts of people, making crude jokes and laughing with them like a common person. His friends gave him advice, saying, 'O King, you should not bring yourself down to things common and undignified. Instead you should sit on your throne all day doing the business of your kingdom. Then the Egyptians would know that they are ruled by a great King.' To them King Amasis gave this answer: 'If you have a bow, you bend it only when you use it. Otherwise you leave it alone. If you keep it bent at all times, it will break. So is it also with a man. If you work without stopping, and don't enjoy sports and good company, you'll get sick, or lose your mind. And because I know this, I do each thing in its own time.'"

Golden statue of the god Amun, 945–712 BC

Here is another historical anecdote about Amasis that we know thanks to Herodotus. "Before Amasis became king, he loved jokes and pranks. Sometimes he drank too much wine and, to make fun of his friends, he stole things from them. His friends suspected theft and, because he didn't admit it, they took him to oracles to find out the truth. Some oracles judged him guilty, but others acquitted him. So when Amasis became king, he stopped paying attention to the oracles that had acquitted him, but those who had declared him guilty of theft, he held in honor as truth-speaking oracles."

Another interesting story that mentions Pharaoh Amasis tells us about the ruler of the Greek island of Samos, Polycrates. Polycrates was a talented leader who turned his island into a wealthy and powerful country. He was friends with famous artists and poets of his day, who flattered him in poems and made gilded statues of him. Amasis heard of the great success and fame of Polycrates and felt a little envious. He wrote a letter to Polycrates in which he suggested that since Polycrates had only good fortune and great success, and not even a single failure, it was a clear sign that one day his good luck would run out and he would end in ruin. To fix this problem Amasis suggested that Polycrates select the most precious thing he owned and throw it away.

Polycrates decided that the advice of Amasis was good. He took his favorite signet ring – an emerald set in gold – and threw it into the ocean. Only a week later a fisherman caught a fish for Polycrates' dinner. Inside the fish he found Polycrates' ring! Polycrates wrote to Amasis asking for more advice, but Amasis concluded that it was impossible to save a man from his fate. Sure enough, soon Polycrates was trapped and killed by the Persians who felt threatened by his growing power.

"The ring returns to Polycrates"

Eventually Amasis himself got into trouble with the Persian Empire as well. Persian 'King of Kings' Cyrus the Great asked Amasis to send him an eye doctor, "the most skilful that there is in the land of Egypt." Amasis found a skilled doctor and forced him to go to Persia against his will, leaving behind his wife and children. The doctor hated Pharaoh Amasis. To teach Amassis a lesson, to show him how it feels to part with one's family, the doctor advised Cambyses (the son of Cyrus the Great) to ask for the pharaoh's daughter in marriage. Amasis didn't want to send his daughter to a foreign land, but he was terrified of the Persians. So, instead of his daughter, he sent to Persia Nitetis, the daughter of Pharaoh Apries, whom he had defeated and allowed to be executed. Needless to say, it was a bad idea! The moment Nitetis saw Cambyses, she revealed the truth to him. Cambyses was enraged and launched an attack on Egypt, but King Amasis had died before Cambuses marched into Egypt.

In 525 BC, Persian troops led by Cambyses II defeated the Egyptian forces led by Pharaoh Psamtik III. Cambyses captured and executed Psamtik III, and crowned himself the Pharaoh of Egypt.

"Cambyses II kills the sacred Egyptian Apis bull"

Cambyses II meets the defeated Pharaoh Psamtik III

This started the 121-year-long period of the First Persian Occupation of Egypt.

In 404 BC, the Egyptians took advantage of instability and civil war occuring in Persia, and threw the Persians out of Egypt, regaining their independence. This period of Egyptian independence lasted for only 62 years. It ended with the defeat of the last native Egyptian king – the last pharaoh of the 30th dynasty – Nectabebo II. After a few years of successfully defending Egypt from the Persians, Nectanebo fell victim to betrayal. Mentor of Rhodes, one of his Greek mercenary commanders, defected to the Persians in 345 BC, taking his forces with him. In addition, several Greek cities agreed to join forces with the Persian 'King of Kings' Artaxerxes III. The Persians defeated the Egyptian forces and installed a Persian *satrap* (governor) to rule over Egypt. Nectanebo escaped south, to Nubia. He is said to have remained there for the rest of his life.

The Second Persian Occupation of Egypt lasted for about 10 years, from 341 to 332 BC. In 332 BC Alexander the Great conquered Egypt. This was the end of the Egyptian dynasties and the beginning of the Ptolemaic Period of Egyptian history, when Egypt was ruled by Greek kings.

ALEXANDER THE GREAT

REIGNED 336-323 BC

During the decades of the Persian occupation, Egyptian culture started fading away. Hieroglyphic inscriptions on temple walls became less common. Religious services were no longer held. Sand buried many temples. Others were looted. The granite colossi of ancient pharaohs were broken and used to construct new buildings.

However, the Persian Empire was about to face an enemy who could not be overpowered or outwitted. Alexander the Great became king of the ancient Greek kingdom of Macedon at the age of 20, and by 30 he turned his kingdom into one of the largest empires in human history, stretching from Greece to India. There are many legends about Alexander. To his contemporaries, and for ages after his death, he looked like a demigod, a hero who brought the light of Greek civilization to lands far and wide. Here are a couple of my favorite historical anecdotes about Alexander. The first comes from the *Moralia – Sayings of Kings and Commanders* attributed to Plutarch.

"Alexander defeats Persian king Darius III at the Battle of Issus" by Pietro da Cortona

In India, Alexander took captive a famous archer, "of whom it was said that he could send an arrow through a finger ring. Alexander asked him to show his skill, but the archer refused. In anger Alexander ordered the man to be executed. As he was being led away, the archer told his guards that he had not practised for many days, and was afraid of failing. When this came to the ears of Alexander, he was filled with respect for the man who would rather die than fail and destroy his reputation. Alexander gave him many gifts and let him go."

The second story was recorded by the 1st-century Roman author Valerius Maximus. "Just as Alexander's bravery in war deserved infinite fame, so his compassion was worth high respect and love. One day, Alexander's Macedonian army was stopped by a snowstorm. As Alexander was sitting in a raised chair near the fire, he spotted an old Macedonian soldier who was shaking from the cold. Alexander came down from his seat, and with those hands with which he had crushed the power of Persian King Darius, he led the frozen soldier to his own seat, saying 'This will be better for you.' Among the Persians, if anyone sits in the king's chair, that person is put to death. Why are we not surprised, then, that Alexander's troops thought it a pleasure to serve their commander, to whom the safety of a common soldier was more dear than the grandness of his royalty?"

"Alexander at the Temple of the Apis Bulls, Memphis" by André Castaigne

In 333 BC Alexander the Great defeated the Persian King Darius III and in 332 BC he marched into Egypt. Most towns on his way capitulated, but the Persian's fortress at the town of Giza refused to surrender. After a lot of bloodshed Alexander took Giza, executed all Persian men of military age and sold all their women and children into slavery. The Persian governor of Egypt surrendered. The Egyptians greeted Alexander as a savior. "For since the Persians had committed offenses against the temples and had governed harshly, the Egyptians welcomed the Macedonians," writes Diodorus Siculus.

Next, Alexander traveled to the oracle of Amun-Ra at the Siwa Oasis. Here is how Diodorus describes this journey: "He came to the desert and began to cross a country covered with an infinite expanse of sand.

After four days they ran out of water, and suffered from terrible thirst. All fell into despair, when suddenly a great storm of rain burst from the heavens. They decided it was due to the action of divine Providence, refilled their water containers from a hollow in the ground, and continued the journey. At one point, their road could not be traced because of the sand dunes. The local guide, however, pointed out to the king that crows cawing on their right were calling their attention to the route which led to the temple."

Describing the Oracle of Amun-Ra, Diodorus says, "The image of the god is encrusted with emeralds and other precious stones, and answers those who consult the oracle in a quite peculiar fashion. It is carried about upon a golden boat by eighty priests, and these, with the god on their shoulders, go without their own volition wherever the god directs them. Many girls and women follow them singing hymns... Alexander walked into the sanctuary and looked at the statue of god for a while. Then the priest who held the position of prophet, an elderly man, came to him and said, 'Rejoice, son! This is how the god wishes to address you.'
Alexander replied, 'I accept, father. From now on I shall be called your god's son. But tell me if your god will give me rule over the entire Earth.' The priest now entered the sacred enclosure and as the bearers of Amun lifted the god and moved according to certain voice commands, the prophet cried out, confirming that the god had granted Alexander his request."
Alexander was crowned King of Egypt in the temple of the god Ptah in Memphis.

"Alexander and his Doctor" – by Eustache Le Sueur (left) and Henryk Siemiradzki (right)
According to Plutarch, Alexander fell sick while on a military campaign in Asia Minor. He then received a letter warning him that Philip, his doctor, had been bribed by the Persians and would poison him. Alexander, however, trusted his doctor. He first drank the medicine prepared by Philip, and then showed him the warning letter.

Alexander's stay in Egypt was brief. In honor of his coronation he organized sports competitions and musical festivals to entertain his new subjects. He also restored a few Egyptian temples, and ordered construction of new monuments to the Egyptian gods.

During his stay in Egypt, Alexander founded the city of Alexandria which became the new capital of Egypt. Diodorus Siculus informs us that Alexander issued a command "to build the city between the marsh and the sea. He traced the streets skilfully and ordered that the city should be named after him – Alexandria. It was conveniently situated near the harbor of Pharos, and by selecting the right angle of the streets, Alexander made the city breathe the sea breezes to provide its inhabitants with a moderate climate and good health. Alexander also laid out the walls so that they were at once extremely large and marvellously strong."

Above: silver tetradrachm
of Alexander the Great
Left: Alexander enters Babylon

In June of 323 BC, as Alexander's troops were marching toward Babylon, Chaldaean astrologers sent messengers to Alexander. "By the configuration of the stars they had learned of the coming death of Alexander in Babylon," writes Diodorus Siculus. "Their messengers told the king that he must not enter the city." Concerned, Alexander sent his friends and generals to Babylon, "but changed his own route so as to avoid the city and set up his headquarters in a camp not far from it... The Greeks were shocked at this act of superstition, and some philosophers came to see Alexander, offering him philosophical arguments against Chaldaean prophecies. The king was convinced and from then on was filled with scorn for all prophetic arts... It was as if the king had been wounded in his soul and then healed by the words of the philosophers, so that he now entered Babylon with his army."

"Death of Alexander the Great" by Karl Theodor Von Piloty

" ...Just when it seemed that he was at the peak of his power and good fortune, fate cut off the
time allowed him to remain alive. Straightway heaven also began to foretell his death, and many
strange omens and signs occurred." A war prisoner, who had been held in chains, freed himself,
escaped from his guards, and sneaked into Alexander's palace. Alexander was taking a bath.
His royal crown and robe were placed on his throne. The prisoner dashed to the throne, put on
Alexander's robe and crown, and sat on the throne. "As soon as the king learned of this, he was
terrified at this odd event. He walked to the throne and, without showing his anxiety, asked
the man quietly who he was and what he meant by doing this." The man didn't say a word.
This event was viewed as a sign that a disaster was about to happen. "Alexander recalled the
prediction of the Chaldaeans and was angry with the philosophers who had persuaded him to
enter Babylon." Soon another ill omen occurred. Alexander wanted to see "the great swamp
of Babylonia" – the marshy delta of the rivers Tigris and Euphrates. When he sailed on the
swamp, he dropped his crown in the water. "One of the sailors swam after it and, wishing to
return it safely, placed it on his head as he swam back to the boat." Alexander's crown kept
being placed on other men's heads!

Sure enough, in a couple days Alexander became very ill, and soon,
at age 32, after 13 years of reign, he was on his deathbed.

It could be malaria he had contracted in the swamps, but none of his friends who had accompanied him were sick, so there were rumors of poisoning. Alexander had no kids. According to Diodorus, "His friends asked: 'To whom do you leave the kingdom?' and he replied: 'To the strongest.'"

When Alexander died, his generals, who were his childhood friends, were first in shock over the loss of their king. But soon they were at each other's throats, fighting for the best pieces of his empire. The province of Egypt fell in the hands of Ptolemy Soter ("Ptolemy the Savior"), one of the seven bodyguards of Alexander. Ptolemy proclaimed himself the governor of Egypt.

Alexander's body was placed in a gold casket that was put inside a gold sarcophagus. A massive funerary cart was built to carry the sarcophagus to Macedonia for burial. However, on the way to Macedonia, Ptolemy seized Alexander's body and had it buried in Memphis. The reason for this action was an ancient tradition, according to which kings in Macedonia claimed their right to the throne by burying their predecessor. Years later, in 305 BC, Ptolemy crowned himself pharaoh and started a Greek dynasty of the kings of Egypt – the Ptolemies.

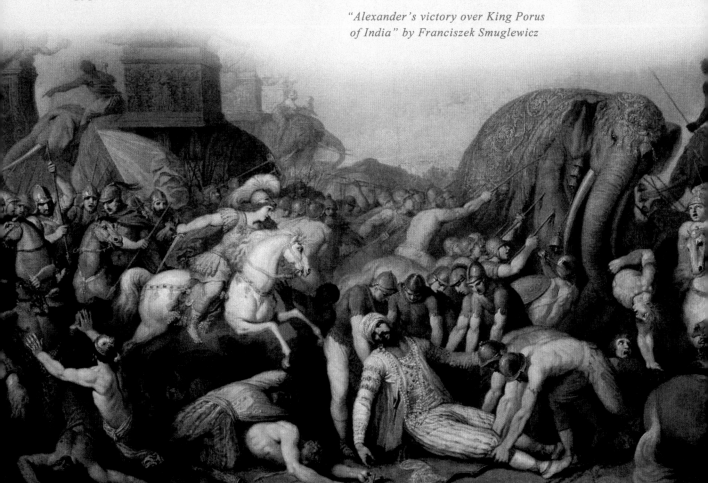

"Alexander's victory over King Porus of India" by Franciszek Smuglewicz

PTOLEMY I

REIGNED 304 – 282

Ptolemy I Soter and his descendants – the Ptolemies – were Greek kings of Egypt who ruled Egypt for about 300 years until the death of Cleopatra – the most famous and the last ruler of this dynasty – in 30 BC.

"Ptolemy took over Egypt without difficulty and was treating its inhabitants with kindness," writes Diodorus Siculus. "Finding eight thousand talents in the treasury, he began to hire mercenaries and to form an army. A lot of friends also joined him because he was honest and just." After decades of wars against the other commanders of Alexander's armies, Ptolemy firmly established himself on the throne of Egypt, ruling from Egypt's new capital – Alexandria. He was a skilled politician and an excellent governor. After humiliation and economic decline under Persian occupation, Egyptians embraced the idea of an independent Egypt ruled by Greeks.

Below: Ptolemy as the pharaoh of Egypt;
"Pharaoh's procession by the Abu Simbel Temple" by Frederick Arthur Bridgman

In Plutarch's "Moralia" we find an interesting report about Ptolemy Soter – a glimpse of his personality. "Ptolemy, son of Lagus, used, as a rule, to dine and sleep at his friends' houses. And when he had parties he borrowed dishes, tablecloths, and even tables from his friends. He himself owned no more than what he needed for everyday life, and he used to say that it was more appropriate for a king to make others rich rather than to be rich himself."

Ptolemy gave financial support to Greek philosophers and scientists who had moved to Alexandria. Among them was the "father of geometry," Euclid, whose famous book, *Elements*, remains the basis of geometry today. Legend has it that King Ptolemy tried to study Euclid's *Elements*, but Euclid's geometry was too hard for him to grasp. So the king asked Euclid if there was an easier way to learn it. Euclid famously replied: "Your Majesty, there is no Royal Highway to geometry." The Royal Highway was a well-constructed and easy-to-travel ancient road that ran across Persia.

mummy mask from the Ptolemaic Period

Ptolemy Soter restructured the Egyptian government. He also rewrote the laws to make them more like the laws in Greece. If an Egyptian wanted to work for Ptolemy's government, he had to learn Greek and adopt Greek customs and traditions.

Alexander the Great's burial procession as described by Diodorus Siculus

Egyptian scarab amulet

The conquests of Alexander the Great spread Greek culture all around the Mediterranean. Greek became the language of international communication. The era that followed – from the death of Alexander in 323 BC to the rise of the Roman Empire in the 1st century BC – is known as the *Hellenistic* period. The word 'hellenistic' comes from Ἑλλάς – Hellas – the name of Greece in Greek.

Ptolemy encouraged the immigration of Greeks to Egypt. Thousands of Greeks from Macedonia, the Aegean islands, and Asia Minor set sail for Alexandria. Greek communities were granted higher status than the towns of native Egyptians. Marriages between Greeks and Egyptians were not allowed. Greek towns were self-governed by councils of elders. The temples of Greek gods, gymnasiums, and Greek schools were built in every Greek village, and the Greek priests and community leaders were free from paying taxes to Ptolemy's government. Ptolemy strengthened the Egyptian army by paying his officers and soldiers with grants of land they could turn into a farm. Large numbers of his soldiers were Greek mercenaries. His cavalry was entirely Greek. The moment Greek soldiers retired from the army, they settled in Egypt, creating a vast class of Greek citizens loyal to the Greek kings of Egypt.

However, despite the arrival of Hellenistic culture in Egypt, Ptolemy and his descendants valued native Egyptian culture and religion, using them to their own advantage. They restored many of the old temples and allowed the Egyptian priesthood to enjoy some privileges.

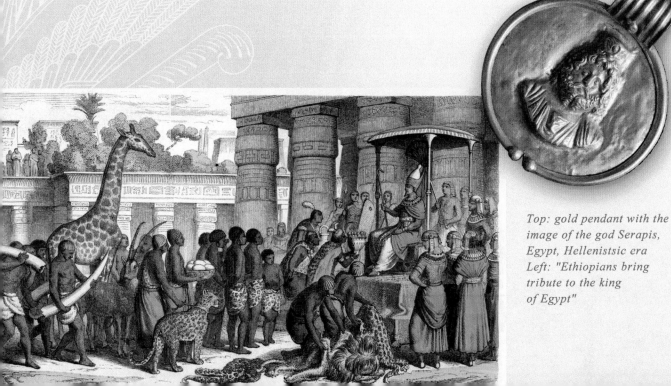

Top: gold pendant with the image of the god Serapis, Egypt, Hellenistsic era
Left: "Ethiopians bring tribute to the king of Egypt"

CLEOPATRA VII
REIGNED 51–30 BC

In the 1st century BC, Rome had become the Mediterranean superpower. By the time Cleopatra VII was crowned the Queen of Egypt, Egypt had become a target for Roman conquest. Rome was still a republic, but within two decades it would become an empire. Egypt couldn't compete with the military power of Rome, but it was envied for its wealth, the luxury enjoyed by its elites, and its spectacular cultural heritage.

In the 1st century BC Alexandria was much fancier than the city of Rome. Rome was surrounded by marshes and plagued by malaria. Its streets were damp, narrow, and reeking of garbage and sewage. Its most famous architectural monuments hadn't been built yet. Alexandria was a well-planned city, with clean water supplied from a man-made lake. It had the Great Library – the largest library of the ancient world, its famous Pharos Lighthouse – one of the seven wonders of the world, a large international community of scholars and scientists, and a vibrant trade and business class. In 58 BC, when Cleopatra was 11, she accompanied her father, Ptolemy XII, to Rome. What did she think of Rome? Probably that it was nothing to write home about!

The weakness of Egypt came from the same source as its strength – the Nile. During the last decades of the Ptolemaic dynasty Egypt experienced extreme droughts. The waters of the Nile didn't rise high enough during the rainy season to provide water for farming. Cleopatra's father increased taxes. That caused riots.

"Cleopatra" by John William Waterhouse

Then he borrowed astronomical amounts of money from wealthy Romans. And that tied the future of the Ptolemies to Rome. In his will, Cleopatra's father Ptolemy XII named his daughter Cleopatra VII and his son Ptolemy XIII as co-rulers. The Roman Republic was named as their guardian. This gave Rome the legal right to step in if Ptolemy's kids refused to play along.

The never-ending cut-throat competition for the throne inside the Ptolemy clan had resulted in a family culture where betrayals, poisonings, and secret murders were an everyday thing. Growing up, Cleopatra learned the skill of eliminating rivals along with other school subjects, such as Greek literature, music, dance, and foreign languages. Ironically, she was the last Ptolemaic ruler and the first one to actually speak the Egyptian language! It was far less useful to her, however, than Latin: Everyone's eyes were on Rome.

Cleopatra and her brother hated each other. Cleopatra looked to secure Roman support to get rid of her brother. Ptolemy XIII was busy doing exactly the same. Meanwhile, in Rome, Pompey and Julius Caesar were engaged in a civil war. As everybody seemed to be distracted with the military action in Italy, Cleopatra suddenly announced herself the sole ruler. Her image appeared on coins. Official documents gave her the title of pharaoh, while her brother was completely ignored. Since Caesar was winning the civil war, Cleopatra's brother decided to get Caesar on his side by 'helping' him. When Pompey, defeated in battle, fled to Egypt, Ptolemy

ordered his murder and sent Pompey's head to Caesar. But Caesar was disgusted by this barbaric act of Ptolemy. His defeated enemy, Pompey, was a fellow Roman citizen whose past victories had brought great glory to Rome. "Arriving at Alexandria just after Pompey's death," writes Plutarch, "Caesar turned away in horror from Theodotus as he presented him the head of Pompey, but he accepted Pompey's seal-ring, and shed tears over it."

Realizing that her brother had made a big mistake, Cleopatra rushed to meet Caesar and win him over to her side.

"Cleopatra welcomes Caesar" by Tancredi Scarpelli

"She was a woman of amazing beauty," wrote Roman historian Cassius Dio, "in the prime of her youth, she was striking. She also possessed a most charming voice and a knowledge of how to make everyone like her. With spectacular looks and the power to charm anyone, she decided to rely on her beauty to support her claims to the throne." According to Plutarch, with only one friend whose name was Apollodorus, late at night, Cleopatra took a boat to the palace where Caesar was staying in Alexandria. To get into the palace unnoticed "she stretched herself at full length inside a blanket, while Apollodorus tied the blanket up with a cord and carried it indoors to Caesar."

Caesar fell in love with Cleopatra right away, but he wanted to drain the Egyptians with civil war, so he demanded that Ptolemy and Cleopatra share power as equals. Ptolemy XIII, in the words of Cassius Dio, "was filled with rage and rushed out of the palace, crying out that he was being betrayed. He tore the diadem – his crown – from his head and cast it away. After this, many battles occurred between the forces of Ptolemy and Cleopatra, both by day and by night, and many places were set on fire, with the result that the docks and Alexandria's storehouses of grain were burned, together with the library, whose volumes, it is said, were of the greatest number and excellence." That's right, the famous Great Library of Alexandria burned when Ptolemy's troops blocked Caesar's ships in the harbor, and Caesar started shooting flaming arrows at the Egyptians in the Battle of the Nile.

Ptolemy's attacks turned Caesar and Cleopatra into allies. In no time Ptolemy was defeated. He drowned trying to escape by crossing the Nile. Cleopatra's older sister, Arsinoe, who took Ptolemy's side, was paraded in chains in a Roman triumph parade, and sent into exile. At that point Cleopatra was 21. Caesar made her younger brother Ptolemy XIV her co-ruler.

For a while Cleopatra and Caesar lived together in the palace in Alexandria. They considered marriage, but both were afraid of offending their people by marrying a foreigner. Caesar had a golden statue of Cleopatra installed in the temple of Venus the Mother, in the Roman Forum.

In 46 BC Cleopatra traveled to Rome. She was an important ally for Caesar because he needed the wealth of Egypt to support his claim to leadership in Rome. However, Caesar's powerful enemies among the Roman elite hated Cleopatra for backing Caesar. Eventually Caesar was assassinated and Cleopatra lost her Roman support.

Egypt was falling apart, torn by riots. Cleopatra tried to win her people back by cancelling taxes, but it was too late. In panic, Cleopatra poisoned her 15-year-old co-ruler brother and, looking for a new powerful friend in Rome, reached out to Caesar's general Mark Antony. They first met in Rome, in 46 BC.

"Cleopatra welcomes Antony in Alexandria" by A.Benini

Plutarch says that is when Mark Antony fell in love with her. "Many times, as he sat in court dispensing justice to tetrarchs and kings, he would receive love notes from Cleopatra on tablets of onyx or crystal. And once, when Furnius was speaking, a man of great worth and the best orator in Rome, Cleopatra was carried through the forum on a chair, and Antony, when he saw her, sprang up from his judge's chair, ran out of the court building, and hanging on to Cleopatra's chair accompanied her on her way."

Five years later she arrived at a meeting with Antony in a lavishly decorated river barge with dancers and musicians dressed as Egyptian and Roman gods. Just like Caesar, Antony could not resist her charm. Also, just like Caesar, he needed Egyptian troops, ships, and money to fund a war against his rivals in Rome.

As expected, Cleopatra offered Antony financial support. In exchange she asked Antony to kill her sister Arsinoe who lived in exile in Ephesus. Arsinoe learned about the plot and fled to the famous Temple of Artemis – believed to be a sacred asylum, where an escaped criminal was not allowed to be seized. However, the assassins caught up with Arsinoe on the steps of the temple and killed her.

Antony came to Egypt and stayed with Cleopatra in Alexandria.

"Antony and Cleopatra watch a theater play" by Alexix Van Hamme

Commenting on his relationship with Cleopatra, Cassius Dio wrote: "She enslaved him so absolutely... that she was called 'queen' and 'mistress' by him. Cleopatra had Roman soldiers as her bodyguards, and all of them had her name inscribed on their shields. Cleopatra followed Antony to the marketplace, joined him in the hearing of lawsuits, and rode with him everywhere. Sometimes she was carried in a chair while Antony accompanied her on foot. He also sometimes wore an oriental dagger at his belt, dressed in a manner not in accordance with the customs of Rome, and let himself be seen even in public on a gilded couch. He posed with her for portrait paintings and statues – he was portrayed as Osiris or Dionysus, and she was portrayed as Selene or Isis. Everybody thought he was bewitched by her through some enchantment, because she charmed not only Marc Antony but also the friends who influenced him. She even seemed to hope that one day she would rule over the Romans..."

Finally, called to suppress a rebellion in Syria, Antony left Egypt. Cleopatra gave him 200 ships for his campaign. There was also pressure from Rome: Anthony's relationship with Octavian, Caesar's heir and his ally, was getting worse and worse.

Octavian divorced his wife, who was Antony's stepdaughter. Her mother, Antony's wife, Fulvia, raised an army against Octavian, but was defeated and exiled. Antony led his troops into battle against Octavian, but their *centurions* – officers who commanded 100-soldier units – refused to fight. For years they had been fighting on the same side, in Caesar's army. How could they fight against one another? Their mutiny forced Antony and Octavian to make peace. Meanwhile, Fulvia died, and, to strengthen their peace agreement, Antony married Octavian's sister, Octavia. That was a disaster for Cleopatra. Destroying Antony's marriage became her main political goal.

Indeed, 4 years later, in 36 BC, Antony and Cleopatra reunited in Syria, and in 34 BC Antony returned to Egypt to celebrate his victory against Armenia. During the celebration he and Cleopatra appeared dressed as a king and queen, and Cleopatra was given the title "The Queen of Kings." Next, Antony sent a letter of divorce to his wife Octavia. Enraged, Octavian broke into the Temple of the Vestal Virgins in Rome where Antony had placed his will for safekeeping. Octavian seized Antony's will and read it in the Senate. According to his will, Antony was going to make the territories he conquered for Rome independent kingdoms and leave them to his sons to rule. He also wished to be buried not in Rome, but in Alexandria, with his queen, Cleopatra. Romans were furious, and declared war against Egypt.

The two fleets – Roman and Egyptian – met at Actium in 31 BC. Antony and Cleopatra suffered defeat, and Cleopatra convinced Antony to secretly sail for Alexandria, leaving their navy behind. "She had reached this opinion as the result of being disturbed by omens," suggests Cassius Dio. "Swallows had built their nest on her flagship... Also, statues of herself and Antony that the Athenians had placed on their Acropolis, had been hurled down by thunderbolts into the theatre, a very bad omen."

"Antony and Cleopatra chose the best of their ships and burned the rest, because so many of their sailors had died of sickness or deserted. Next, they secretly put all their most valuable possessions on board by night, and left for Alexandria."

Octavian chased them to Alexandria and sent word to Antony ordering him to commit suicide. As for Cleopatra, he wanted to take her to Rome to make her walk in chains across the city during his triumph victory parade. Roman historian Marcus Velleius Paterculus describes the end of Antony and Cleopatra:
"Antony promptly ended his life...Cleopatra tricked her guards and had an asp (a venomous snake) smuggled in to her. She ended her life by its venomous sting."

"Death of Antony" by Louis Moritz
Below: "Cleopatra receives snakes hidden in a fruit basket" by Victor Eugene Delacroix

Octavian, now Caesar Augustus, seized control of Egypt, and it became a Roman province. Roman rule in Egypt lasted from 30 BC to 359 AD when the Roman empire was divided into two parts and Egypt became a province of Byzantium, the Eastern half of the Roman Empire.

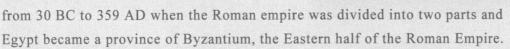

As Roman historian Tacitus put it,
"It seemed wise to keep under the direct control of the emperor
a province which produces great harvests,
but has a problem of riots and civil wars
because of the fanaticism and superstition of its inhabitants
who are ignorant of laws
and unfamiliar with the principles of elected government."

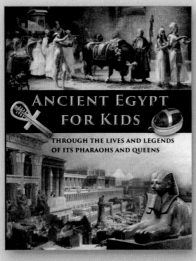

ANCIENT EGYPT FOR KIDS

THROUGH THE LIVES AND LEGENDS
OF ITS PHARAOHS AND QUEENS

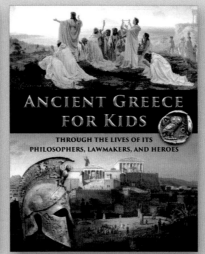

ANCIENT GREECE FOR KIDS

THROUGH THE LIVES OF ITS
PHILOSOPHERS, LAWMAKERS, AND HEROES

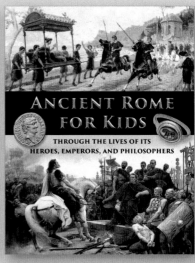

ANCIENT ROME FOR KIDS

THROUGH THE LIVES OF ITS
HEROES, EMPERORS, AND PHILOSOPHERS

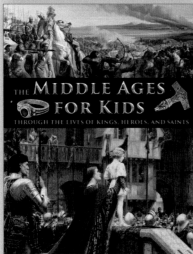

THE MIDDLE AGES FOR KIDS

THROUGH THE LIVES OF KINGS, HEROES, AND SAINTS

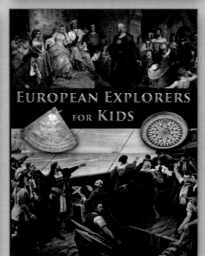

EUROPEAN EXPLORERS FOR KIDS

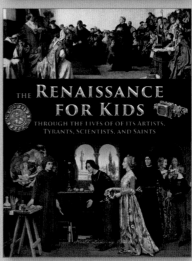

THE RENAISSANCE FOR KIDS

THROUGH THE LIVES OF ITS ARTISTS,
TYRANTS, SCIENTISTS, AND SAINTS

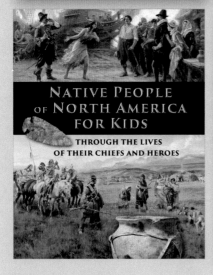

NATIVE PEOPLE OF NORTH AMERICA FOR KIDS

THROUGH THE LIVES
OF THEIR CHIEFS AND HEROES

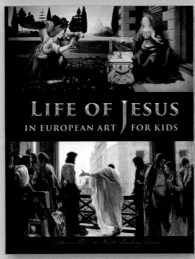

LIFE OF JESUS

IN EUROPEAN ART FOR KIDS

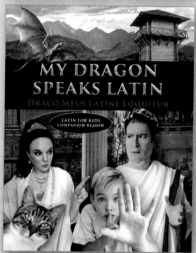

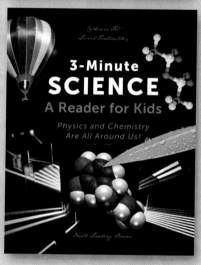

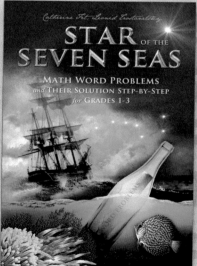